The 9th Life of Felix The Cat

Awakening Your Greatness: Lessons Learnt From Eight Wasted Lives

By

Robert N. Jacobs
MSC

All rights reserved
Copyright © Robert N. Jacobs, 2025
The right of Robert N. Jacobs to be identified as the author of this
work has been asserted in accordance with Section 78
of the Copyright, Designs and Patents Act 1988
The book cover is copyright to Robert N. Jacobs
This book is published by
Growth Seeker Publishing Ltd.
www.growthseekerpublishing.com

This book is sold subject to the conditions that it shall not, by way of
trade or otherwise, be lent, resold, hired out or otherwise circulated
without the author's or publisher's prior consent in any form of binding
or cover other than that in which it is published and
without a similar condition including this condition being imposed
on the subsequent purchaser.
This book is a work of fiction. Any resemblance to
people or events, past or present, is purely coincidental.
ISBN: 9798281051262

To my incredible daughter, Ava.

Life is not about avoiding mistakes or discomfort but about embracing them with courage, curiosity, and authenticity. Like Felix, never settle for mediocrity; live bravely, passionately, and unapologetically. Be guided by your faith, your integrity, and your heart, and never let the noise of the world drown out your voice.

Foreword

You are holding a book that could change the way you approach your life. In these pages, you will follow the curious and profound journey of Felix the Cat, a creature just like you, longing for something beyond the ordinary. Each of his first eight lives felt wasted, sabotaged by fear, comfort, procrastination, approval-seeking, aimlessness, regret, distraction, and mediocrity. Yet you will see how he finds the determination to rise above these pitfalls, culminating in a ninth and final life where every lesson finally clicks into place.

When you dive into Felix's story, you will embark on your own parallel journey. You will discover that fear need not paralyse you, that endless comfort breeds stagnation, that procrastination drains your most precious resource—time, and that approval-seeking buries your unique voice. You will recognise the danger of drifting without a vision, the gnawing pain of regret when you do not act, the subtle poison of losing focus in a busy world, and the quiet lull of settling for "just enough." More importantly, you will see how to conquer each of these traps through simple, powerful shifts in your mindset and daily actions.

This book stands apart because it goes beyond telling you what to do. Through Felix's lives, you will see the real consequences of poor choices—and the staggering possibilities that open up when you reclaim discipline, courage, and urgency. You will be inspired to banish hesitation, unleash untapped skills, and build a life where every day pulses with meaning. As you turn these pages, your perspective will sharpen. You will begin to see that no matter how much time has slipped by, real transformation starts the moment you decide to live fully and boldly.

My aim is for you to reach the end of this book fired up and unwilling to let your own precious days slip into mediocrity. Let Felix's final life ignite your passion for living. Let his lessons unlock your potential. Most of all, let yourself dream bigger, act braver, and love every step of the journey. This is your invitation to awaken the greatness that lies within you. Read on, and be ready to discover how your next chapter can shine brighter than you ever imagined.

Robert Jacobs
Curious By Design

Table of Contents

The First Life

Fear 1

    Fear's Invisible Chains 2

    The Origins of Fear 6

    Fear's Impact on Potential 10

    Philosophical Insights on Fear 14

    Breaking the Cycle of Fear 18

    Conclusion of First Life 21

The Second Life

Comfort 23

    Escaping Fear, Embracing Comfort 24

    How Comfort Narrows Your World 27

    The Lull of Complacency and Its Consequences 31

    Waking Up From the Comfort Slumber 34

    The End of Comfort: Felix's Second Death 38

    Conclusion of Second Life 40

The Third Life

Procrastination 42

    The Lure of "I'll Do It Later" 43

    Root Causes of Procrastination 46

    Procrastination's Impact on Potential 49

    Philosophical Insights on Procrastination 53

    Breaking the Cycle of Delay 56

    Conclusion of Third Life 59

The Fourth Life

Seeking Approval 61

- The Trap of External Validation 62
- Why We Crave Acceptance 65
- The Cost of Living for Approval..68
- Philosophical Insights on Authenticity 72
- Breaking Free from the Need for Approval 75
- Conclusion of Fourth Life 79

The Fifth Life

Aimlessness... 81

- The Quiet Drift into Aimlessness..82
- Why We Avoid Purpose 85
- The Consequences of Living Without Direction 88
- Philosophical Insights on Purpose....................................91
- Rekindling Focus and Meaning 95
- Conclusion of Fifth Life...98

The Sixth Life

Regret 100

- The Shadow of Missed Opportunities.............................101
- The Anatomy of Regret..104
- How Regret Stifles Growth..107
- Philosophical Reflections on Regret...............................111
- Transforming Regret into Resolve 113
- Conclusion of Sixth Life..117

The Seventh Life

Distraction 119

A Thousand Shiny Distractions 120

Why Distraction Feels So Appealing 123

The Cost of Fragmented Attention 126

Philosophical Perspectives on Distraction 129

Rekindling Depth and Focus 132

Conclusion of Seventh Life 136

The Eighth Life

Mediocrity 138

The Comfort of the Ordinary 139

Why We Settle for Less 142

The Unseen Cost of Living Below Potential 145

Philosophical Insights on Rejecting the Ordinary 148

Choosing Excellence Over the Comfort Zone 150

Conclusion of Eight Life 153

The Ninth Life

Your Last Life 155

The Urgency to Live Boldly, Bravely, and Unapologetically 156

The Daily Habits of Highly Effective and Impactful People 159

Leaving a Lasting Legacy: How to Ensure Your Life Truly Matters 163

Tying It All Together: Lessons from Lives 1-8 167

The Final Awakening: Embracing Your Last Life's Legacy 171

Conclusion   175

"Life is not a rehearsal; it's the performance; don't spend it waiting backstage."

Robert N. Jacobs

THE FIRST LIFE

Fear

You find yourself in a world where nine lives seem like an endless gift, yet time has a way of slipping through your paws. Meet Felix, a cat who faces the same uncertainties and hesitations you do. In his first life, Felix is plagued by fear. He knows there is more to existence than scurrying along alleyways and curling up in the safest corners, but the thought of risking his comfort terrifies him. Hissing dogs, intimidating tomcats, and unpredictable humans create an environment where his instincts scream at him to hide rather than explore.

Yet behind Felix's timid eyes, there is a longing for discovery. He senses that cowering in the darkness robs him of the richest parts of being a cat. He watches bolder felines vault fences, claim entire gardens as their own, and stroll across rooftops without glancing down. Part of him yearns to experience that same freedom. Another part shudders at the idea of leaping into the unknown. So, he remains in the shadows, letting fear dictate his every choice.

This chapter follows Felix as he grapples with his first life of fear. You will see how invisible chains lock him away from his potential, how fear takes root in his past experiences, how it stifles his growth, how timeless wisdom can help him shift his mindset, and which practical steps can finally break fear's hold. Yet, by the time Felix masters these lessons, his first life draws to an end. He conquers fear too late, missing the chance to flourish before this life closes. That final breath leaves you a powerful reminder: do not wait as long as Felix did. Face your own fears now, and make every life, every chance, truly matter.

Fear's Invisible Chains

Picture Felix in the early hours of dawn. He's crouched behind a bin, whiskers trembling. He can smell a half-eaten tin of tuna on the other side of the alley. It's probably delicious, and he's starving, but fear whispers that the territory might be guarded by a fiercer feline. His stomach aches, yet the thought of confrontation overwhelms him. Rather than risking it, he ducks back into the dark, missing what might have been a rewarding meal.

These moments happen regularly for Felix. Small choices, like approaching an unknown cat or venturing into a new street, become monumental in his mind. The hiss of a cornered rat or the rumble of a passing lorry can send him running to the nearest hiding place. On the surface, it's just caution, but you know it goes deeper. Felix has formed a habit of avoiding anything that carries a hint of risk. His every move is shackled by invisible chains.

You might wonder how a cat could be so paralysed by fear. Survival instincts are part of every feline's nature, yet Felix's anxiety goes well beyond self-preservation. He has missed out on promising food sources, safer sleeping spots, and friendly encounters that might enrich his life. Over time, these missed chances have moulded Felix into a timid cat, prone to seeing danger in every corner. Rather than wandering through gardens or across rooftops, he stays in confined areas he knows, letting life pass him by.

Fear

These chains do not clang or rattle; they're silent, created by his own thoughts. Fear paints vivid pictures of fierce dogs, territorial cats, or sudden squalls that could leave him exposed. Because his first impulse is to shrink back, he rarely questions whether these threats are real or inflated by his imagination. The more he flees, the more his world shrinks until nearly every street is off-limits. This is the subtle power of fear's invisible grip.

Many cats are drawn to curiosity, sneaking through open windows or scaling fences to discover hidden pockets of the world. Felix, however, feels only the weight of dread at each new sight or sound. He sees bolder felines crossing wide roads, exploring human gardens, or chasing dragonflies in open fields. Though he admires their bravery, he has convinced himself that such feats are well beyond his capacity. He thinks, "If I'm not certain I'll come out safe and sound, I'd best not try at all."

As the nights pass, Felix finds himself mewing with a quiet yearning. He knows there must be more to being a cat than mere survival. He aches for a sense of adventure, for unexpected moments of delight, a chance at fresh fish left out on a windowsill, or a new vantage point high on a rooftop. Sometimes, he imagines napping on a soft blanket in a kindly human's home. Yet each time he contemplates stretching beyond his known territory, fear's phantom leash tugs him back.

Fear wears many disguises in Felix's life. Sometimes, it poses as a caution, whispering that he must stay alert because the world is threatening. Other times, it calls itself realism, convincing him that crossing into new areas is a fool's errand.

In truth, much of what holds Felix in place comes down to untested assumptions. He rarely checks whether the big tom in the adjacent alley is truly hostile or if the barking dog in that fenced garden is even there. Felix's decision to keep to the same few streets ensures he never challenges these assumptions.

You might feel your own experiences reflected in Felix's story. Where you shy away from giving a presentation, Felix huddles behind a bin. Where you dread asking for a promotion, he dreads stepping into the alleyway controlled by a larger cat. The specifics differ, but the outcome is the same: you both remain stuck, tethered by worry, missing out on the unknown rewards that come with venturing forth.

There's a deep irony in fear's invisible chains. They promise safety but deliver a narrower, lonelier existence. Felix is rarely in direct harm, yet he's also deprived of the joy, companionship, and self-belief that grow from overcoming trials. Over time, he barely even remembers what it feels like to be excited or curious. Each new squeak, each shifting shadow, simply evokes another wave of dread.

This first step in Felix's journey is to notice these chains. He begins to ask himself why he always runs from the slightest threat. Is the world truly so dangerous, or is he caught in a loop of imagining the worst-case scenario? His instincts, honed by experience, argue that keeping hidden is wise. However, a small spark in Felix's mind insists that he was meant to do more than cower. This spark lights the path ahead, the path that will invite Felix to dismantle fear's hold. Yet that path is treacherous, for it demands new habits of thought and action.

In your own life, naming these invisible chains is a bold move. Instead of pretending everything is fine or that you're simply "not that kind of person," you acknowledge that fear might be running the show. Like Felix, you might be dodging potential joys because you're fixated on potential dangers. By bringing these patterns into the open, you start loosening their grip.

However, identifying fear is just the first step. Breaking free requires a willingness to question your assumptions, to test them in reality. For Felix, that could mean inching a little further down the alley each day, observing whether the threats he imagines ever materialise. For you, it might involve sharing an idea in a meeting or asking a question you've been too nervous to ask. These early attempts are small, but they represent a dramatic shift in who you believe yourself to be.

Felix's story in this first life is about slowly discovering that he is not as fragile as his fears suggest. Gradual experiments, investigating a new corner, and interacting with a passing feline instead of running bring small revelations. He starts to see he can withstand awkward moments or uncertain outcomes. Most of the dire threats he envisioned do not occur. This realisation starts to thin out the dense fog of anxiety that has overshadowed him.

In time, Felix even dares to approach a kindly human who sets out a bowl of milk near a back door. Heart pounding, he creeps closer instead of retreating at the first creak of a footstep. To his amazement, the human doesn't chase him away. This first taste of milk outside his usual streets hints at what might be waiting if he pushes beyond his comfort zone. It marks a subtle but significant turning point: the notion that new experiences might be worth the risk.

These minor victories accumulate. They alter Felix's self-image, inch by inch. He realises that he is not doomed to be a scared cat scurrying through the shadows. With every step taken despite fear, he discovers an alternative storyline. Courage, it seems, does not require being fearless. It merely asks that he move forward even though his whiskers tremble.

Of course, the chains remain. A single bold moment doesn't dissolve a lifetime of hiding. But each time Felix opts to challenge his boundaries, he chisels at fear's foundations. The cracks deepen. He might still freeze at unexpected sounds or run at the sight of a larger cat, but it happens less often. As his confidence grows, so does his appetite for fresh experiences.

Yet the clock of this first life ticks on. While Felix makes incremental progress, his days are finite. No matter how carefully he claws his way past anxiety, time marches forward. He is on his first life, with eight more to come, but he remains unaware of how fleeting this particular span will be. The lessons he learns here, spotting fear's invisible chains and realising they can be broken, will carry him forward, but not before life number one ends.

The Origins of Fear

If you observe a kitten in a safe home, it often seems fearless. Little ones bat at anything that moves, chasing strings, pouncing on unsuspecting tails, and climbing curtains without a second thought. Over time, though, experiences teach caution. A harsh encounter with an unfriendly dog, a sibling that hisses and swats, or a fall from a high place can plant the seeds of anxiety. Felix's story begins in a similar way. In his earliest memories, he scurried around with barely a care until reality taught him to fear.

You might ask why fear clings so tightly. Part of it lies in feline instincts. Cats are predators but also prey for larger animals. Evolution has shaped them to stay alert and avoid unnecessary risks. If you let your curiosity drag you into a fox's den, your life could end abruptly. Fear, in the wild, is a lifesaver; it keeps a cat vigilant, ensuring it isn't caught off guard by something bigger and stronger.

Yet Felix's environment isn't quite that brutal. He is in a suburban neighbourhood with more dustbins than foxes and more humans than lurking predators. Still, his ancient instincts flash a red light at every unknown. When the shadows move at dusk, he's not sure if it's a passing cat or something more dangerous. So he slinks off and hides rather than investigate. His evolutionary heritage has primed him to suspect danger, even if the odds are low.

Personal history adds a layer. Early experiences matter. If Felix encountered nasty run-ins with bigger felines when he was a kitten, that memory lingers, reminding him that vulnerability can be punished. A cat that has been cornered or beaten up might forever see confrontation as too risky. When the memory of past pain is vivid, future challenges appear far more daunting. Felix learned this the hard way. He once ventured onto a roof, slipped, and tumbled into a rubbish bin. Though he escaped mostly unharmed, the episode shook him to the core. He concluded that venturing into unknown spaces is rarely worth the hazard.

Social influences also play a subtle part. Felix observes how other cats behave. If he sees them hissing at outsiders, forming rigid territories, he learns that the world is a patchwork of zones to be guarded and contested. The local feline code might be strict: cats who cross boundaries risk a fight. Over time, Felix internalises the idea that nearly every new space is a potential battlefield. Instead of forging alliances or exploring, he stays put, worried he will trigger conflict.

In your own life, you might see parallels. You watch how peers handle challenges, glean messages from family experiences, and shape your worldview around past failures. Before you know it, you're convinced that stepping out of line is sure to end badly. For Felix, each hiss or claw encountered as a younger cat solidified his belief that unknown territory is best avoided.

Another layer is the modern environment, full of strange sights and loud noises. Lorries rattling by, children running up driveways, humans slamming car doors at odd hours. As a cat, Felix can be startled by these unexpected interruptions. A quiet street can suddenly erupt with commotion. In such moments, his flight reaction takes over, sending him scurrying for cover before he even knows what's happening. Fear becomes his default setting, a reflex cemented by repeated jolts of panic.

Unpicking these strands helps you understand Felix better. He's not foolish or lazy; he's responding to instincts, memories, and signals that shaped him long ago. What once served a practical survival role has grown out of proportion in his modern surroundings. This is the catch: fear can overstep its useful boundaries, keeping a cat from discovering beneficial experiences. It stops being a safeguard and becomes a prison.

Felix's deeper struggle also ties to the notion of identity. After spending so long in fear's clutches, he starts to believe that timidity is part of who he is. He sees confident cats strutting through open windows or scaling fences without flinching, and a small voice inside him says, "That is not me." Identifying as a shy cat feels safe but also limiting. It permits him to stay within his comfort zone, though he often yearns for a richer existence.

When he peeks out of the alley to watch others roam more freely, Felix sometimes wonders if he's missed a crucial lesson. He's aware that not every cat is fearless. Some simply manage to face their uncertainties in exchange for better meals, warmer homes, or livelier companionship. Their gambles pay off often enough that they continue taking them. Felix, however, never tests such odds. That consistent avoidance means he rarely collects evidence contradicting his fears.

Understanding the origins of fear in Felix's life underscores one key principle: fear is not always a sign that you are incapable or weak. It is an understandable response that can sometimes overreach. In practical terms, it's fine for Felix to be wary of a snarling dog, but it's less helpful for him to remain paralysed long after the dog has been leashed and led away. His repeated experiences taught him that unknown equals dangerous, even when the danger has passed or was never truly there.

You might identify with the sense that what once protected you is now confining you. Lessons you learned about the world through experiences, warnings, or cultural norms might be outdated. Yet they remain lodged in your mind, prompting you to overestimate threats while underestimating your capacity to adapt. Felix lives at the mercy of his past. His instincts, shaped by an environment that demanded constant vigilance, no longer serve him as effectively in his suburban setting. Without consciously revisiting these old conclusions, he remains stuck in fear's loop.

In the quiet intervals, Felix ponders whether his caution is truly justified. He's never returned to that rooftop where he once slipped. He avoids certain streets just because of a single encounter when he was small. The more he thinks about it, the more he realises that some of those dreadful dangers might have receded or changed. But habit is a strong force. It takes effort to question what feels like second nature.

Ultimately, Felix is starting to glimpse that fear, while valid in principle, may not always be grounded in present realities. To make genuine progress, he'll need to challenge the old rules his experiences taught him. Rather than blindly trusting his flight instinct, he must find new ways to assess the world around him. This is where his journey truly begins. Yes, fear shaped him, but maybe, just maybe, he can reshape himself. That fresh awareness sets the stage for exploring what fear does to his potential.

Fear's Impact on Potential

Imagine Felix stands on a gate at dusk, peering over into a spacious garden. He smells chicken scraps, hears mild rustles in the shrubs, and feels the pull of curiosity urging him to leap down. Yet fear asserts that a canine might lurk behind every bush, or a territorial cat might be on guard. Felix hesitates for ages until he backs away in defeat. He slinks off, hungry, toward a safer spot he's visited a hundred times before. Here, you see the quiet tragedy of fear: it can bar you from the very experiences that might enrich and expand your life.

Potential, in Felix's case, is not just about finding better meals. It includes forging alliances, discovering warm nooks, enjoying a sunlit nap on a fence post, or befriending humans who offer comfy laps and steady meals. Fear erects an invisible barrier, ensuring he experiences only a fraction of what the feline world has to offer. As you watch Felix, you might sense a parallel in your own life. Where he misses out on a new garden, you might miss out on new roles, adventures, or connections because you freeze at the threshold.

Over time, fear carves out a smaller and smaller zone of safety. Felix trudges the same few streets, convinced that deviation spells trouble. This repetitive pattern robs him of the simple thrill that so many cats treasure: exploration. Cats are known for their curiosity, but Felix's is stifled. The confidence he might have developed as a hunter or a roamer is replaced by an identity dominated by timidity. His world shrinks, and with it, his sense of who he can be.

The heartbreak is that Felix isn't lazy or unambitious. He yearns to do more; he sees glimpses of the life he might lead. Yet fear's nagging voice overshadows the call of possibility. He imagines the worst: bigger cats blocking his path, humans shooing him with loud noises, or unsteady ledges from which he might tumble. These images are so vivid that they feel more real than any potential success or joy.

In your life, you may feel a similar pull between the future you want and the fear that tells you it's too risky. You might sense a creative spark, a desire to lead, or a craving for adventure, but avoid stepping forward because you believe it will end poorly. Fear shrinks your potential by urging you to remain small, untested, and safe. Like Felix, you might experience pangs of regret, realising what you let slip by.

Another outcome of fear is the decline in self-belief. Each time Felix sees a daring cat prancing along a fence, he thinks, "That could never be me." He has not gathered evidence of his own ability to conquer precarious ledges or face off with mild threats. So, each missed attempt strengthens his feeling of incapacity. Eventually, he believes wholeheartedly that he cannot handle the bigger challenges in life. This becomes a self-fulfilling prophecy: you don't act because you feel weak, and you remain weak because you don't act.

Moreover, fear robs Felix of the relationships that could elevate his existence. Cats, while independent, can form bonds with each other, with friendly humans, or even with other animals. These connections often lead to warmth, companionship, and mutual security. Terrified of rejection or confrontation, Felix avoids forging these bonds. Loneliness sets in as he watches from a distance, envious of felines basking in the sunlight beside a caring owner, or strolling with cat friends through a backyard playground.

When fear dominates, each new situation is viewed through the lens of what could go awry, not what might flourish. Felix's mind references every small misfortune from his past, painting a future that seems doomed. Success becomes an outlier, not the norm. Hope grows dim. He might even resent cats who appear unafraid, blaming them for having it easier. In truth, many bold felines have faced their own hazards. They've simply decided that the rewards outweigh the risks.

Yet there is a way out of this cycle. If Felix musters enough curiosity to take a few calculated steps past his comfort zone, he'll learn that fear is often exaggerated. The dog he expected might be sleeping indoors. The big tomcat might not be guarding the fence at all. The shrub hiding the scraps might be empty of threats. One successful venture could inspire a second, then a third. Over time, Felix might realise that he's capable of coping with uncertainty, and he'd gather proof that fear lied to him.

These truths also apply to you. The voice of fear can sound convincing, but real confidence grows from facing the unknown. Without testing your abilities, you can't dispel the illusions that paint you as powerless. Breaking away from stagnation starts with a decision that your potential is worth the inconvenience of anxiety. Each time you move forward, you reclaim a part of yourself that was buried under layers of self-doubt.

For Felix, small, brave steps might involve scoping out a new route at twilight when streets are quieter. He might greet a fellow cat in neutral territory, seeing if the cordial meow is returned. He might push open a barely ajar door, exploring a back garden to locate fresh water. Step by step, he reclaims pockets of the neighbourhood that he'd long avoided. Each success proves that his fear-fuelled imagination often paints the world as harsher than it really is.

Nonetheless, these breakthroughs don't happen overnight. Felix must battle the reflex to scurry away at the first sign of unpredictability. This is where resilience is formed. Each time he confronts a surprise, whether it's a mild scolding from a human or a startled bark from a dog next door, he has the chance to learn that he can handle such events and bounce back. That lesson might be the key to unlocking his real potential.

In the end, the biggest tragedy is if Felix waits too long and never explores the fullness of his first life. Fear can siphon off the best of any creature's existence if left unchallenged. The sooner Felix acts, the sooner he discovers that his potential extends beyond rummaging through one or two safe bins. A bigger universe lies just over the fence, and it's available to those prepared to face the short-term discomfort of uncertainty.

Unfortunately, fate is unyielding. As Felix musters the courage to broaden his horizons, time marches on. The first life has limits. He can glean insights about fear's impact on potential and even start to break free, but he doesn't realise how close his final moment in this body might be. Overcoming fear at the last gasp offers a bittersweet victory: yes, he proves he's capable, but that realisation arrives just as life number one slips away.

Philosophical Insights on Fear

Even a cat's world resonates with timeless wisdom. Think of philosophers who observed that suffering arises when you focus on what's beyond your control. Felix can't halt every canine bark or hush every passing car, yet he allows these external forces to dominate him. Stoic viewpoints, if you translated them into feline terms, might tell him to direct energy toward his own actions, his willingness to explore or his decision to stand his ground rather than fret about every possible disturbance.

Existential thinking might remind Felix that each choice defines his essence. He is not only the product of instincts or territory but also the sum of actions he dares to take. Every time he edges onto a new fence or into a new backyard, he's forging a path that expands who he is. Fear tries to deny that freedom, telling him that his destiny is fixed. Yet existential perspectives remind him he has the freedom to shape his life within certain constraints, and this truth can be both frightening and liberating.

Mindfulness, in a cat sense, might involve Felix learning to be present in each moment: feeling the breeze ruffle his fur, sensing the ground under his paws, and observing the subtle changes in scent around him. Fear thrives when Felix leaps ahead in his mind, imagining catastrophic run-ins. By noticing the here and now, he might realise that no immediate danger lurks in every shadow. While vigilance is useful, panic often arises from speculation rather than fact.

Philosophically, fear can also serve as a teacher. If Felix's biggest worry is being chased off territory, it reveals he values security and acceptance. Recognising that can help him approach new areas with a sense of purpose: he's seeking a safer, more fulfilling existence. He might even team up with a friendlier cat, realising that an alliance can bring both security and companionship. Rather than seeing fear as only an obstacle, he can see it as highlighting what truly matters.

Across many traditions, there's a notion that you suffer more in imagination than in real experiences. Felix exemplifies this when he sees a rustle in the weeds and dashes away, picturing a hulking threat. The dread is real, but the threat might not be. Cats who adapt well accept that a certain level of caution is healthy, but indefinite retreat is not. There's wisdom in trusting that you can respond to circumstances as they arise without pre-emptively shutting down all possibility.

Community can play a powerful role, too. Cats are sometimes solitary, but they do form colonies or alliances under the right conditions. If Felix found supportive companions, cats willing to defend each other or share safe spots, he'd discover that not every hiss is an attack. Philosophically, this suggests that fear is partially dismantled by real connections. Isolation amplifies worry; fellowship offers perspective. Other cats might show him hidden paths, safe vantage points, or reliable feeding spots, all of which reduce the unknown.

This is where the universal appeal of such teachings emerges: even you, as a human, can relate to how fear warps reality. If you treat every new event as if it's guaranteed trouble, you limit your scope before you ever test the waters. Philosophical frameworks encourage you to see yourself and your decisions with fresh eyes. They remind you that anxiety, while natural, need not define the rest of your life. The cat who tries remains open to growth, while the cat who surrenders to fear grows stale and regretful.

In stepping back to reflect on these principles, Felix begins to piece together a different approach. He acknowledges that he can control only his own movements, not the world's every twist and turn. He sees that if he yearns for comfort, he must risk introducing himself to new places or beings that could bring exactly the comfort he craves. He realises that living perpetually in the future, imagining all possible calamities, robs him of the immediate present, which is frequently calmer than his anxious mind predicts.

It won't be a seamless transformation. Felix is a cat of habit, shaped by evolutionary caution. But these philosophical insights give him a context to interpret his life differently. As he starts to test new waters, he replaces guesswork with lived experience. When an outcome is challenging, he learns from it; when it's rewarding, he gains courage. Either way, he steps beyond the stale territory fear had confined him to.

Crucially, philosophical wisdom suggests that fear itself can become a stepping stone. Each burst of anxiety reminds Felix what is at stake: a chance for nourishment, connection, or personal growth. When he feels that nagging worry, he can see it as a prompt, a sign that something significant might lie on the other side of his reluctance. By braving that boundary, he might discover aspects of the world or himself he didn't know existed.

The question remains: will Felix apply these lessons quickly enough to enjoy a long, fulfilled first life? Or will his realisation dawn too late, giving him only a moment of triumph before that life's clock runs out? In many philosophical teachings, time is an ever-present theme. You cannot halt its passage, so each delay has consequences. Felix is learning truths that could revolutionise his life, but the moment to act is now, not tomorrow.

As the sun rises on another day, Felix reflects on what he's gleaned. He's still nervous, but he sees a path forward. Trust in his own agility and resourcefulness. Seek alliances. Explore with a touch of caution rather than total paralysis. Accept that the world moves in unpredictable ways, but that he can handle more than he once believed. These insights empower him to attempt changes he never would have dared in the past. Whether these changes bear fruit in time for him to enjoy this life remains to be seen.

Breaking the Cycle of Fear

By now, you see how Felix is entangled in fear's many layers. He's identified the silent chains, uncovered how they formed, recognised their toll on his potential, and even gathered some philosophical outlooks. The final question is how to translate all this understanding into decisive action. Practical steps are essential if Felix is to break fear's hold before this first life slips away.

Exposure is one such strategy. Instead of hiding when faced with a new environment, Felix tries to inch closer each time. If there's a yard he's never ventured into, he starts by peeking through a gap in the fence. He waits, observing quietly, noticing if any real threat materialises. His muscles tense, but he resists the urge to flee at the first sign of movement. Over repeated tries, he sees that no monstrous creature leaps out. That revelation alone dissolves a chunk of his dread.

Cognitive reframing also helps Felix challenge his dire assumptions. When he spots an unfamiliar shape on the pavement, he intentionally questions the worst-case scenario swirling in his head. Could it be a friendly cat? Or a harmless bin bag? Is running away the only choice? By training his mind to ask these questions, Felix gradually lessens the reflexive terror that once ruled him. Even if the shape turns out to be a curious dog, he's better prepared to gauge the actual danger rather than blindly assume disaster.

A mindful approach grounds Felix in each moment. Instead of being lost in hypothetical horrors, he tracks his breathing and the sensations of his surroundings. His whiskers pick up subtle shifts in the air; his ears scan for genuine threats rather than imagined ones. If he feels anxiety spike, he labels it: "Fear is here." Then, he decides what to do rather than letting fear command him. This practice is neither fancy nor complicated, but it allows him to stay in reality rather than in anxious speculation.

Social ties become a surprising ally. Cats are known for independence, but a few friendly felines live nearby. They've occasionally extended a meow of greeting, but Felix used to slink away. With a spark of newfound courage, he responds in kind. Over time, he discovers that supportive companions can ease tension. One cat might show him a safe route onto a shed roof. Another might help chase off an actual threat. This unity replaces some of Felix's isolation with a sense of belonging.

Of course, the road is uneven. Felix has nights when a strange noise spooks him so badly that he bolts back to his familiar hiding place. The old habits run deep; one or two experiments won't erase them instantly. What keeps him going is the knowledge that each slip-up is part of the learning curve. When he panics and flees unnecessarily, he later reflects: "Next time, I'll pause before running." That vow helps him do a little better the following day.

Rewarding himself with simple pleasures also cements his progress. After venturing onto a new fence, Felix might discover a vantage point with a warm patch of sunlight. He savours that moment, realising it's a direct result of facing his alarm. This positive association transforms risk-taking from a purely terrifying ordeal into something that might yield comfort, nourishment, or entertainment. These small joys become powerful motivation.

Such incremental victories accumulate, slowly reshaping Felix's identity. No longer does he see himself as a helpless cat cringing at every bump in the night. He's evolving into a feline who, while still cautious, can push boundaries when needed. Each success stands as proof that fear's dire predictions often fail to match reality. Courage is building, not from a single heroic act, but from a steady flow of smaller confrontations that reveal his untapped strength.

All of this is crucial because time is short. Felix doesn't realise it, but his first life's end draws near. Still, with every step forward, he embraces more of the world. He discovers tidbits left behind by kindly humans, warm spots beneath windowsills, and the rush of curiosity that emerges when he plays with other cats in a communal garden. These are glimpses of what life could have been all along had fear not caged him.

In your own journey, these tactics, exposure, reframing thoughts, mindfulness, support networks, and celebrating small wins can shift you from paralysis to progress. Fear may still rear its head, but you learn to interpret it differently: a signal that you're stepping into new territory rather than a command to retreat. Gradually, you prove to yourself that you can adapt to uncertainty. This shapes a more resilient self-image, one in which potential becomes bigger than dread.

Yet, there's a bittersweet note to Felix's triumph. He finally understands that he can face fear and that he can survive awkward or precarious moments. He's nibbling at fresh experiences, forging playful bonds with fellow felines, and discovering that much of the dread he carried was an illusion.

He has, in essence, conquered the first life of fear. But precious time has run its course. Just when Felix is poised to enjoy this newfound freedom, an unexpected moment seals his fate in this life, perhaps a misjudged leap or an unforeseen threat that he never truly anticipated.

You might see this as tragic: Felix overcame his fear, only to have his days cut short. But there's another angle. His final breath in this life is not marked by the old terror. Instead, he departs with the knowledge that growth was within his grasp all along. This realisation, though fleeting, plants a seed that will awaken when he comes back in his second life. The lessons of fear and courage won't vanish but remain etched into his memory. The next life holds fresh challenges, but Felix will no longer be the same quivering cat he once was.

Conclusion of First Life

Felix spent much of his first life bound by fear, hiding in dimly lit corners and missing out on the wonders around him. He learnt, at the eleventh hour, that he held the power to question his assumptions and step beyond his self-made boundaries. Just as he tasted the thrill of living free from constant dread, his first life ended. Had he been bolder sooner, he might have claimed more sunlit fences, enjoyed cosy laps, and formed deeper bonds with fellow cats. Still, he departs this life with vital insights that will resonate in the next.

You've watched Felix progress from paralysed caution to a fragile confidence, revealing how deeply fear can distort your reality. You've seen that gradual exposure, reframing worried thoughts, leaning on supportive connections, and fostering a spirit of mindful curiosity all carve a path out of fear's grip. The tragedy is that Felix discovered his courage too late to enjoy a contented existence in his first life. Yet it's also a reminder of how crucial it is to act now rather than waiting for a final moment of epiphany.

When Felix awakens in his second life, he'll recall the lessons from this one. He'll no longer be the cat who cowers at the slightest rustle. Instead, he'll face the next set of challenges with a readiness born of hard-won knowledge. Fear might be subdued, but new pitfalls lurk on the horizon. The life of comfort will have its own perils and distractions, threatening to dull Felix's sense of possibility. Nevertheless, the cat who left this first life behind did so enlightened and unafraid. Remember his story as you reflect on your own obstacles. Don't let fear steal your potential. Seize each moment while you still can because no life lasts forever.

The Second Life

Comfort

You may think that once you have beaten fear, life becomes free and easy. That is how Felix, the cat with nine lives, starts his second incarnation. Freed from the crippling anxiety that defined his first life, he emerges with a fresh sense of boldness. Fear is no longer an anchor, and Felix now roams with quiet confidence. Yet, in this new existence, the absence of terror leads him into an unimagined problem: the life of comfort.

At first, being comfortable feels like the perfect antidote to fear. Felix no longer cowers at shadows or runs from every sound. He grows relaxed, untroubled, and content in familiar surroundings. This might sound ideal, but a different kind of trap begins to form. With no sense of urgency pushing him forward, Felix becomes less inclined to explore or seek anything beyond what is readily available. Food is within easy reach, safe spots are abundant, and catnaps fill his days.

You will follow Felix as he savours this existence, believing he has finally found peace after the strain of his first life. Gradually, though, the comfort zone tightens around him like a snug collar he cannot see. Friends move on, opportunities pass him by, and Felix finds himself stuck in a pleasant but uneventful routine. While complacency might be soothing, it also drains vitality and growth. By the time Felix realises what he has lost, his second life is dangerously close to its last chapter.

In this instalment, you will see how comfort can be as limiting as fear, how it begins subtly, how it constricts the edges of possibility, how timeless wisdom can help you rediscover your spark, and why decisive action is needed before life slips away again. Watch as Felix learns these truths the hard way, just before this life ends.

Escaping Fear, Embracing Comfort

Imagine Felix opening his eyes to a new dawn. Gone is the timid cat who once trembled at the creak of a bin lid. In the early phase of his second life, he wakes refreshed, stretching luxuriously in the warm glow of morning light. He feels neither threat nor suspicion, and that alone is a revelation. For so long, fear governed his every step, urging him to hide and stay small. Now, curiosity and relief replace those tense instincts.

This initial confidence serves Felix well. He roams the streets without second-guessing every shadow. He strolls by barking dogs with only a passing glance, no longer imagining worst-case scenarios. Boldness injects vitality into his movements. Unlike before, he might investigate a new corner of the neighbourhood or rub against a stranger's leg without flinching. These moments bring a rush of pleasure as Felix savours the freedom that comes with conquering fear.

At first, you might see this as the beginning of a triumphant arc. Freed from the chains of worry, Felix appears ready to seize any opportunity he encounters. Yet, comfort soon finds its way into this story. You might ask: how can comfort be a problem for someone who recently battled crippling fear? The answer lies in the human (or feline) tendency to seek security once immediate threats subside. Felix's mind, relieved of anxiety, starts favouring the easiest paths. He naps in the same cosy spot, accepts meals from the same friendly human, and finds no compelling reason to wander further.

There's a delicate line between enjoying life's comforts and becoming reliant on them. In small doses, rest and simplicity can be deeply restorative, especially after an existence dominated by tension. However, once Felix's immediate challenges vanish, he drifts into a lull. Gone is the spark that drove his final moments of the first life, when he dared to reclaim lost ground. Now, he carries no fear but also no drive to push beyond the safety of known routines.

In this phase, Felix displays a subtle complacency. Where he once made tiny efforts to broaden his horizons, he now thinks, "Why bother?" If warm milk is readily provided, why hunt or forage? If a cushioned patch of grass is always available, why risk discovering a brighter patch somewhere else? Before long, Felix's daily routine reduces to three central pursuits: food, dozing, and grooming. The same cycles repeat, day after day.

You might see parallels in your own life. After overcoming a major hurdle, maybe finishing a challenging project or conquering a personal phobia, you may shift into a comfortable rhythm. It feels deserved, especially if you have come from a place of hardship. Yet the mind can grow addicted to comfort, dulling the instinct to aim higher. Before you realise it, weeks or even years can pass in this pattern of doing just enough to feel content without forging ahead.

Felix's relationships also reflect the comfort trap. While other cats might still roam or explore, Felix often lets them come to him. He never denies them company, but he seldom initiates a new venture. If a fellow cat suggests investigating a distant park, Felix yawns and wonders what use that would be. Over time, his social circle contracts as more ambitious felines move on to bigger territories, leaving Felix behind with a shrinking number of friends. He is not exactly unhappy, but a faint restlessness begins to creep in.

Comfort also affects physical health. Without the impetus to explore or hunt, Felix becomes plumper. His muscles lose their old tautness, and while he may not notice it immediately, agility starts to decline. Danger might be a distant rumble, but if it emerges, Felix is now slower to react. By living in a plush bubble, he's lost some of the sharp instincts that once served him well, even if they were overshadowed by fear.

At this stage, you could still defend Felix's lifestyle as a deserved respite. Indeed, it is natural to take a break after profound stress. The issue arises when a pause turns into a permanent halt. Felix stops learning, stops pushing boundaries, stops discovering new aspects of himself or the world. In short, he quits growing. His mind and body rest on the status quo, satisfied with just being comfortable. This can be deceptively alluring. After all, there is no pressing problem or obvious pain, so why change anything?

Yet, life is dynamic; it rarely supports endless stagnation without eventual repercussions. In the next section, you'll see how the comforts Felix has grown to love begin eroding possibilities, weakening his sense of purpose. While he may not yet recognise the problem, the seeds of decline have been planted. You might reflect on times you felt content and drifted, only to wake up one day to see how much time or opportunity had slipped away.

Felix's second life starts with the opposite scenario of the first: no crippling fear, no anxiety nightmares, no nervous vigilance. It is a sweet, calming reprieve. However, if he stays in this mode indefinitely, he risks another form of unfulfillment. Oddly enough, a lack of external challenges can lead to its own brand of emptiness. The comfort zone keeps him blissfully numb to any drive for improvement. Unless he jolts himself from this cocoon, he risks looking back with regret, wondering if he wasted another precious life by settling too soon.

You might see the paradox: fear locked Felix out of life, but comfort can do the same. One is a negative barrier, the other a deceptive lull. Both can prevent authentic growth. It's at this point that Felix's second life takes shape. Unaware of the danger, he rests on the soft grass, lulled into a slow slide toward mediocrity. The question remains whether he'll notice in time to change his path or whether this calm existence will become a silent killer.

How Comfort Narrows Your World

After you achieve a sense of security, the mind often ceases to crave expansion. This is precisely the predicament Felix faces in his second life. Freed from the urgent need to fight or flee, his horizon paradoxically shrinks. He chooses the gentlest routes, the easiest meals, and the coziest corners. At first, that seems harmless, but over time, comfort silently erects its own walls. By opting for guaranteed ease, Felix gradually loses sight of what else might be out there.

Walk with Felix through his daily routine. He wakes in a sheltered spot under a tree, where a shaft of sunlight warms his fur. A friendly human sometimes places a dish of cat food nearby, meaning Felix need not hunt or venture far for nourishment. The local dogs have grown indifferent to him since he rarely roams near their territory. Nearby cats come and go, chasing birds or rummaging through bins, but Felix is content to observe from a distance. Day drifts into night, and night cycles back to day without challenge or urgency.

This comfortable pattern reduces Felix's environment to a small radius he rarely leaves. His world no longer pulses with the excitement of discovery or the satisfaction of tackling a problem. While it is free of conflict, it also lacks that spark of energy that once pushed him to test his boundaries. You see, comfort narrows your world by convincing you there is nothing worth pursuing beyond what you already have.

You might have felt something similar if you have ever settled into a reliable routine after a stressful period. Perhaps you had plans or goals, but once you entered a phase of stability, your ambition gently fizzled out. The same job, the same hobbies, the same circle of acquaintances, these can feel perfectly fine, until you realise years have rolled by without any new growth. You might find your senses dulled, your curiosity fading, or your memories blending into one long blur of routine.

For Felix, the consequences become noticeable when he tries to recall his past. The first life, though fraught with fear, had moments of bright awakening. He can remember that single leap of courage into a new alley, the heart-pounding thrill of tasting freedom. Now, ironically, the absence of adversity leads to days that look the same. He naps under the same tree, eats the same food, and hardly moves beyond the same few metres of ground. The everyday merges into a single, hazy recollection.

Complacency has other hidden costs. You might think that by avoiding tension, you protect yourself from harm, but that also leaves you unprepared for inevitable challenges. If Felix's cosy shelter is knocked over by a storm, or his friendly human moves away, he lacks the resourcefulness to adapt. Without practice in responding to new scenarios, he risks panic or disarray the moment his bubble bursts. Comfort robs him of the resilience that comes from grappling with uncertainty.

Opportunities for adventure also fade. Felix has grown so used to convenience that he ignores signs of something bigger. A neighbour's garden might have a pond brimming with fish, but he cannot be bothered to investigate. A kindly person might invite him indoors, but he is too accustomed to his tree spot to relocate. Each passing chance silently disappears, leaving Felix with the same safe patch of grass, the same daily routine.

If you project this idea onto your own life, you might notice that comfort can sabotage your next level of success or fulfilment. Without any internal drive, you never step up to bigger tasks or more meaningful connections. While you may avoid stress in the short term, you also avoid the spark of transformation. The path narrows, until your world is a fraction of its possible size, and you risk spending your days drifting rather than really living.

Felix's friendships feel this pinch too. Other cats, still curious about broader territory, invite him along, but he shrugs, convinced there is no need to stray. Over time, those friendships wane. While nobody overtly severs ties, the camaraderie that comes from shared exploration dissolves. Felix lingers in his comfort zone, while his peers gather fresh stories of distant rooftops or hidden passages behind old sheds. Eventually, they forget to stop by, certain that Felix is too settled to join in.

Meanwhile, Felix's physical condition continues to soften. Without the impetus to climb fences or track small prey, his muscles weaken. The older cats around him still enjoy short bursts of agility, but Felix is perpetually resting, grooming idly, or enjoying a snack. His new curves and slower reflexes barely register as problems because he faces no immediate threat. Yet, just as the mind dulls when it lacks stimulation, the body grows inert without challenge.

Comfort narrows his perception in yet another way: the acceptance of mediocrity. Felix might once have taken pride in being quick on his paws or cunning in a tricky situation. Now, those ambitions seem irrelevant. He rarely needs to be quick or cunning if everything is laid out for him. While he experiences no pressing misery, he also feels no driving satisfaction in his daily life. A quiet emptiness grows, even if he cannot yet name it.

This pattern might continue indefinitely, except for the quiet discontent that nags Felix now and again. Perhaps a distant memory of how exhilarating it felt to conquer a fear resurfaces. Or he spots an adventurous cat returning with a tale of the big pond or meeting humans who provide a warm fireplace on cold nights. Briefly, Felix's whiskers twitch with interest. Then he shrugs and resumes his comfortable routine, giving in to the inertia he has allowed to take over.

By keeping him untested, comfort stunts his development and blocks potentially wonderful experiences. The tricky part is that it doesn't feel like a severe problem in the moment, so change rarely happens. You likely recognise a version of this in your own life: the slow slide into routine until something or someone forces you to ask if you're missing out. For Felix, the unfortunate reality is that this question arises only when it's almost too late to matter.

The Lull of Complacency and Its Consequences

The transition from healthy relaxation to complacency is often so gradual that you barely notice it. That's precisely how Felix drifts into a state of near-permanent idleness during this second life. At first, he deserved a rest after the turmoil of his fear-driven existence. A few weeks of easy living turned into months, which turned into a languid lifestyle with no expiry date in sight. If you asked him, "Isn't there more you could explore?" he might tilt his head and wonder why you'd disturb his peace.

Yet there's a cost to this unchallenged existence. Complacency, in essence, is an internal choice to stop seeking growth. It is driven by the belief that where you are is good enough, so why try harder? If nobody pushes back, if no threat looms, you stay where you are. For Felix, this means sleeping longer, stretching less, and feeling little need to sharpen his instincts. While he avoids stress, he also forfeits the potential that adversity might awaken.

You might think complacency at least keeps him free from trouble. However, it also leaves him ill-prepared for the unplanned. When a new cat arrives in the area, a bold, assertive fellow with intentions of claiming local food sources, Felix is caught off guard. He has grown so used to having a safe supply of treats that he's never thought about defending or securing it. The newcomer, sensing an easy takeover, edges in. Felix, startled by the intrusion, doesn't know how to respond. He tries a weak hiss, but his intimidation factor is close to nil. Before long, the new cat has taken Felix's favourite resting spot. Felix, the cat who once overcame fear, passively surrenders this territory, all because he has grown complacent and out of practice.

Complacency also affects Felix's emotional engagement with life. He rarely feels true excitement or genuine connection these days. His daily routine, though comfortable, leaves little room for wonder. He might watch a bird flutter overhead and recall a time he felt the rush of chasing prey, but now he can't stir the energy to pursue anything unless it practically falls at his paws. The result is a bland contentment that offers neither highs nor meaningful achievements.

In your own life, complacency might show up as declining new projects at work because you're content with current duties. You might stick to the same social circle, turning down invites that could broaden your horizon. Perhaps you tell yourself that what you have is enough, which can be a valid viewpoint. The danger lies in using that rationale to avoid any stretch that might enrich your existence. Over time, you risk losing the spark that drives growth, the inquisitiveness that once made life feel dynamic.

At a deeper level, complacency can mask regrets. Felix occasionally feels pangs of guilt when he observes other cats returning from daring escapades with shining eyes and new stories to share. A quiet question gnaws at him: "Am I missing something?" But because he isn't overtly suffering, Felix easily dismisses that question with a shrug. The path of least resistance remains appealing, and so he pushes the discomfort aside.

Physically, the consequences continue to pile up. Felix's once-graceful form is now heavier, his reflexes blunted by inactivity. If a sudden threat does appear, a dog barking too close, a car reversing into the driveway, he scrambles with clumsy moves that display how out of shape he's become. While he escapes harm for now, the warning signs are there: he's losing the edge that once gave him confidence. Life might be calm, but it is also precariously balanced on his declining agility and untested resilience.

This second life of comfort also stifles curiosity. You might recall how, in his first life, Felix eventually discovered that braving new territories yielded surprising rewards. Even though fear delayed that discovery, it finally gave him a reason to push his boundaries. Now, with comfort as the norm, Felix sees little incentive to move beyond his immediate circle. The thirst for exploration, dulled by routine, fades more with each passing day. Complacency slowly suffocates creativity and interest in the unknown, leaving behind a cat who is simply marking time.

Yet the world continues to shift, often in quiet, unnoticeable ways. The local environment evolves, cats migrate, and humans change their habits. Felix's static approach fails to account for these external shifts. By the time he realises that his once-reliable food source is drying up, or that new cats have overtaken his favourite territory, it's too late to react effectively. Complacency never taught him how to adapt quickly, so he's left at a disadvantage.

On an emotional level, Felix also drifts from any sense of purpose. During his final days in the first life, he at least had a mission: to conquer fear before his clock ran out. Now, in the second life, he has no mission, no greater aim that pulls him forward. Days bleed into each other, and he can't muster enthusiasm for anything beyond immediate indulgences. This is the hidden downside of a life free of stress: without occasional tension or goals, complacency becomes a dead-end.

The final blow arrives unexpectedly, as it often does. Felix realises, too late, that he needs to hustle when a sudden crisis unfolds. Perhaps the kind human who fed him every day moves away, leaving him without the easy meals he depended on. Or a local authority clears the lot where he sleeps, forcing him to relocate. Felix, unaccustomed to doing much of anything, struggles to cope. His attempts at hunting fail; his search for a new refuge is clumsy. By the time he feels the urgency to adapt, his second life is already at risk.

Complacency, it seems, can be just as lethal as fear, albeit in a quieter way. Felix avoided the extremes of terror but also slipped out of readiness and motivation. He never felt the sting of panic, but he left himself vulnerable to the slow erosion of purpose. In the next section, you'll see how cats (and you, in your own life) might snap out of this lull. Yet for Felix, the question is whether he'll muster that change in time or whether this second life will end with no real accomplishments besides a series of leisurely naps.

Waking Up From the Comfort Slumber

The turning point often arises when you glimpse how much you stand to lose by staying too comfortable. For Felix, this wake-up call arrives in the form of a mild calamity. The human who once left him food every morning departs, leaving an empty house behind. A fence is erected around the property, shutting off Felix's carefree access to his favourite bowl and sun-warmed porch. Overnight, his simple routine is shattered. Suddenly, the leftover scraps he'd come to rely on vanish, and the space that felt like home is off-limits.

Your own life might share a similar jolt. Perhaps a project you assumed was secure is downsized. Or a key person in your support system moves away. Whatever the trigger, you realise how you've grown dependent on unchallenging comforts. In an instant, you feel the ground shifting beneath your feet, forced to adapt when you're out of practice. The panic is less about fear of the unknown and more about the shock of losing what you took for granted.

Felix, caught off guard, tries to navigate the unfamiliar situation. He prowls the perimeter of the new fence, meowing in confusion. He searches half-heartedly for another food source, but the neighbourhood has changed since he last explored. A younger, leaner cat has claimed the prime spots behind a nearby restaurant, and Felix's attempts to scrounge are met with cold stares. He attempts to climb onto a low wall for a vantage point, only to discover he's grown heavier and less agile. He slips and lands with a painful thud, shaken by how unfit he has become.

This rude awakening stirs a sense of urgency. Felix realises he can no longer rely on his old comfort zone. For the first time in his second life, he feels a pang of regret about his long slide into complacency. He wonders how things might have been different if he'd kept exploring, kept forging alliances, and maintained a sharp mind and strong body. He feels nostalgic for the fleeting moments of boldness that crowned his final weeks of the first life.

Yet, regret alone isn't enough. What Felix needs now is a plan. He remembers how, in his first life, the shift from fear to courage involved small steps and gradual challenges.

Perhaps the same approach could help him escape the pitfall of comfort. If you were in his position, you might begin by examining one corner of your routine that has grown stale and seeking a minor but meaningful change. Felix, for instance, forces himself to walk further each morning in search of scraps from different bins. He aims to rebuild his agility, one careful leap at a time.

As Felix reawakens his curiosity, he starts noticing details he previously overlooked. There's a newly built shed in a neighbour's garden, possibly housing mice. A different street has an elderly human who sets out food for strays once a week. By searching beyond his old boundaries, Felix feels a small thrill reminiscent of the discovery he tasted at the end of his first life. It's not as dramatic or laced with fear, but it still invigorates him.

He also realises that forging connections could help. Those fellow cats he once ignored are now potential allies. In reaching out, Felix learns that some of them have formed a loose network, warning each other of aggressive dogs or sharing knowledge of feeding spots. Swallowing his pride, he apologises for dismissing their invitations in the past. Though cautious, they allow him to tag along on a scouting mission. Felix's sluggish pace and lack of stamina make him a liability at first, but at least he's trying. That show of effort restores a glimmer of their respect.

In your own realm, the path out of comfort might follow a similar pattern. You start by shaking up your habits, joining new groups, or seeking fresh challenges. The initial steps can be daunting because you realise how much ground you've lost, but each small success rekindles self-belief. Over time,

Comfort

you remember the satisfaction that comes from pushing your boundaries, not just resting within them.

A crucial element is self-awareness. Felix acknowledges that he let complacency overtake him, so he takes responsibility for his current predicament. Rather than sulking about the fence, he can't cross, he invests energy in building the skills he neglected. He practices short bursts of running, climbing slightly higher walls each week, and reintroducing a bit of hunting instinct to sharpen his reflexes. These routines are tiring, but they stir a deep sense of pride he forgot he could feel.

Felix also stops living in the past. He can't reverse his months of idle living, but he can shape what remains of this life. Although he doesn't recognise the fleeting nature of his nine lives, a part of him senses that each life can slip away if not used well. This urgency lights a fire under him, motivating him to reclaim his sense of purpose. He realises comfort can be a fine resting place, but it should never become a permanent hideout.

As he rebuilds his strength, Felix gains a fresh sense of autonomy. He's no longer reliant on that one human's routine, nor is he stuck beneath the shadow of the new fence. The world feels bigger again, and each small victory fuels his determination. Yet, he must remain vigilant. The second life is already deep in its course, and no cat can live forever. It's not enough to wake up from comfort's slumber; you must also make the most of the time you have left.

In the final section, you'll see whether Felix can recover quickly enough to truly thrive in this second life or if it will slip from his grasp before he experiences the rewards of a balanced existence. Either way, you'll gain insight into the importance of not drifting too far into complacency, lest your days vanish in a haze of unremarkable ease.

The End of Comfort: Felix's Second Death

Time creeps forward in ways Felix barely tracks. Despite his newfound resolve, he has lost precious months, maybe years, to a cycle of laziness and routine. Although he's begun to move with purpose again, an undercurrent of regret flows through him. You may recall moments in your life when, after a long period of complacency, you tried to catch up, only to realise that some chances had already passed. Felix is in a similar position now, racing against an invisible clock.

He invests his remaining days in building friendships, learning new foraging routes, and restoring his agility. These efforts pay off in small, satisfying ways. He relocates to a more vibrant part of the neighbourhood, where humans leave occasional treats and other cats share scouting tips. Each dawn, he sets a goal, perhaps scaling a higher fence or seeking a new vantage point. While these activities might sound mundane, they restore Felix's sense of progress.

Yet, the second life is winding down. Felix notices subtle changes: the once-lustrous fur around his muzzle now has a peppering of grey, and his energy wanes sooner in the day. Where he used to run across rooftops in short bursts, he now must pace himself. He realises that comfort not only softened his mind; it also contributed to an ageing body that didn't get enough exercise to stay fit. Though he's more capable than before, his second life's decline has started.

A stroke of misfortune seals his fate. One afternoon, as Felix attempts a daring leap onto a high window ledge, his rear legs fail to propel him with the force he needs. Perhaps years of inactivity took a toll on the muscles, or perhaps it's just the unstoppable march of time. He falls, landing awkwardly on hard concrete. In a flash, pain radiates through his limbs. A startled meow escapes him, but no immediate help arrives. The second life is close to its final breath.

As he lies there, Felix reflects on the lessons he has learned. Comfort, while soothing, can be a potent trap. It seduces you into a life free of trouble but also free of growth. He realises that if he had maintained even a fraction of his curiosity and initiative, his body might have stayed strong enough to prevent this accident. More importantly, he would have lived a fuller, more engaged second life. The loss he feels isn't just about the injuries; it's about the opportunities he passed by, all because life was pleasant enough to remain stagnant.

In your own journey, you might take this as a stark reminder that complacency can harm you when inevitable challenges arise. If you never test your limits, you lack the resilience to handle surprises. While you may not face a dramatic fall like Felix, you could discover that your mental or emotional muscles have weakened from disuse when life demands more of you. The moment you need them most is precisely when you regret letting them atrophy.

Felix's final moments in the second life are unexpectedly peaceful. Despite the physical pain, he feels a strange calm wash over him. He thinks of the bold cat he was at the tail end of his first life and the content yet stagnant cat he became during the peak of his second. He sees how in striving to avoid all stress, he lost his drive to pursue anything worthwhile. A tiny flicker of comfort returns in the sense that he understands the mistake: letting complacency rule unchecked.

An awareness dawns that this lesson will carry over to the next life. He may be powerless to save this body now, but the experiences remain etched in his essence. His eyes flutter shut, and with a gentle sigh, Felix passes on. This second life, so leisurely at its height, ends not in triumph but in a humbling realisation: rest and ease, when taken to excess, can breed unpreparedness and regret.

You might find Felix's farewell bittersweet, as he did gain some joy from a comfortable existence. Yet the real tragedy is how late he recognised that comfort can be as limiting as fear, draining the chance for discovery and evolution. The final breath of his second life echoes a call to never settle into complete complacency. There is a difference between resting well and refusing to grow.

Conclusion of Second Life

Felix's second life began in a realm free from panic and strife. After surmounting fear, he slipped into a world of easy naps and reliable meals. You may have recognised the allure of such a life, especially after enduring a season of hardship. Yet, as the days rolled on, that cosy routine became a quiet prison. Felix, lulled by comfort, ceased to seek new paths or maintain his edge. In the end, he could not summon the strength or resilience to extend his days.

This chapter reveals the danger of living without an incentive to strive. Whether you are a cat or a person, comfort can dull the senses, corrode the drive to create and connect, and leave you exposed when the environment eventually shifts. Felix learned that soothing circumstances if left unchallenged, undermine the vitality and preparation needed for the future. His final moments arrived too soon for him to live in the balance of relaxation and purposeful living.

As he steps into his third life, Felix will carry these lessons in his memory. He will recall that while fear can paralyse you,

Comfort

comfort can lull you into inaction. Both states lock you away from an existence that brims with potential. The third life brings its own theme, its own pitfalls, and its own chance to rewrite his story. The question is whether Felix will apply what he has learned in time. Will he manage to avoid the extremes of dread and complacency, forging a more fruitful path? Continue following him on this journey, remembering the cautionary tale of how easily comfort, like fear, can lead to an unfulfilled end.

The Third Life

Procrastination

You have followed Felix the cat through two lives already. In the first, he was paralysed by fear, letting anxieties dictate his every move until he learned, at the last second, to act more boldly. In the second, he sank into comfort, drifting in easy routines that eroded his will to explore. Both times, Felix's life ended before he could fully apply his newfound insights. Now, in his third incarnation, you might think he is finally ready to strike the right balance. Yet, a new hindrance awaits him: procrastination.

Freed from crippling fear and from the pull of endless comfort, Felix awakens in this third life with a sense of opportunity. He recalls lessons from his past existences, feeling a fresh desire to do more and live well. But soon, he notices a peculiar pattern. Each time a task or challenge presents itself, a small voice in his mind purrs, "You can do that later." Rather than leaping into action, Felix finds himself stalling over trivial details, napping away precious hours, or wandering off before seeing anything through.

This chapter highlights how delay can be as damaging as outright fear or complacency. By putting off key moments or decisions, Felix gradually wastes the potential he was so determined to use. Through five subheadings, you will see how procrastination starts innocently, why it tightens its grip, how it throttles growth, which philosophical ideas shed light on the problem, and the steps required to break this damaging cycle. Although Felix's memory carries fragments from his first two lives, he still risks repeating old mistakes, only this time by forever pushing action to "tomorrow." Will he notice what is happening before his third life ticks to its end? Turn the page and watch as Felix grapples with the silent yet powerful habit of procrastination.

The Lure of "I'll Do It Later"

Picture Felix greeting his third life with an eager heart. He has some dim recollection of how fear and comfort led him astray, so now he wants to live more wisely. Early in this new existence, he pads around with a sense of resolve, thinking, "I must not waste this life." Perhaps he aims to find the best possible territory, make friends, or discover unknown corners of the neighbourhood. Yet, at each turn, a quiet whisper persuades him, "There's no rush. Start tomorrow."

At first, it feels harmless. After all, Felix has nine lives, or so he believes, and this third one still seems fresh. He can afford a day or two to rest, gather his thoughts, or wait for the weather to improve. When a fellow cat suggests exploring a lively park, Felix nods with enthusiasm but decides to wait for better conditions. When he eyes a promising gap under a garden fence, he thinks, "I'll slip through there after I get more energy."

This dynamic might sound familiar. The temptation to postpone tasks is rooted in the belief that you have plenty of time. Each moment of delay feels minor, just a day, just a moment, just a short rest, yet these minutes accumulate. Felix, realising he is no longer fearful or stuck in comfort, sees no immediate harm in waiting. In that sense, procrastination seems like the gentlest of vices. It doesn't sting like terror or lull you like total comfort; it merely nudges you to push important things to "later."

Yet, as the days turn into weeks, Felix begins to sense a pattern. The tasks on his mental list remain undone. He hasn't scouted that hidden garden or formed the alliances he hoped would keep him safe and active. Instead, he finds small distractions everywhere. A patch of sunlight, a butterfly worth stalking, a friendly human leaving out scraps. None of these are bad in themselves, but collectively, they derail his bigger plans.

You might experience your own version of this. You intend to tidy up a cluttered room, but you decide to do it "after one more hour of rest." Or you vow to learn a new skill, but you wait for the perfect day. Over time, these delays morph into months, then years, leaving you with a sense of wasted potential. The real danger lies not in one instance of postponement but in allowing a habit of delay to build.

For Felix, the immediate consequences are subtle. He still manages to eat, sleep, and roam. There is no crisis forcing him to act, so a half-hearted existence feels oddly acceptable. Now and then, a voice inside prods him, "Shouldn't you be doing something else?" But it is easily silenced by the reassuring thought, "Tomorrow will be better." The cat who overcame crippling fear no longer leaps from hiding spots, but he also does not leap into purposeful action. He drifts along on a raft of good intentions, forever anchored to the same old spot.

Eventually, a friend tries to remind Felix of his potential. Another cat, named Sable, has noticed Felix's aimless pattern. She meows that there is a newly opened pathway through a fence leading to a small orchard filled with fresh prey and interesting scents. Felix listens politely, imagines how delightful that orchard might be, and then mumbles something about needing to rest his legs. He promises to join her "soon," though he cannot pinpoint when "soon" actually is. Sable departs, and he remains behind, aware he is missing out, yet unwilling to stir himself at that moment.

This is the insidious side of "I'll do it later." You hold onto the idea of taking action, which soothes any guilt, but you never commit to a specific time. As a result, you feel that your plans remain feasible while also avoiding the effort of pursuing them. Felix now drifts from day to day, always meaning well, always intending to do something more, yet never quite starting.

A common misconception is that procrastination equals laziness. But in many cases, like Felix's, it is driven by a mix of hesitation, perfectionism, and the belief that future you will be more motivated or prepared. Felix might think he needs the "perfect moment" to explore that orchard or bond with new feline friends. He convinces himself that once conditions align, a pleasant day, an empty stomach, the right mood, he will pounce on these opportunities. Meanwhile, time ebbs away, and he remains stuck in inaction.

Now and then, Felix experiences moments of clarity. He recalls that in his second life, too much comfort led to regret. He thinks, "I must not let that happen again." But the voice of procrastination always counters with a seductive promise: "You won't. You'll definitely do it, just not right now." This promise reassures him that he is not truly repeating past errors, effectively pushing the day of reckoning further down the road.

By highlighting these details, you see why procrastination can be so potent. It appeals to the best parts of you, your desire for things to be done well, your hope for ideal circumstances, and twists them into excuses for postponement. Felix, lulled by the idea that he is preserving his energy for a perfect day, fails to notice that no such day arrives. The more he delays, the more his tasks and dreams pile up, forging an invisible wall of inertia.

In your own life, you might identify with Felix's gentle but persistent cycle of "not yet." It feels harmless in the short run and even comforting, since you believe you are in control. Yet the hours or weeks pass, and you watch ambitions remain half-baked. Real progress seldom happens while you wait for the elusive "right time." A healthier approach involves tackling tasks in the here and now, accepting that conditions are rarely perfect.

Thus begins Felix's third life: free from fear, free from total comfort, yet strangely stalled by the whisper of delay. He might not yet recognise the severity of procrastination's grip, but as you read on, you will see how this habit tightens, preventing him from making use of the lessons he carried over. Without realising it, Felix may be on the path to another untimely end, having squandered his days on the idea that tomorrow will always be there.

Root Causes of Procrastination

Where does procrastination truly come from? You might think it's just a casual tendency to be idle, but there are deeper reasons why Felix, or you, might repeatedly put things off. In Felix's case, several hidden triggers propel him toward delay. Understanding these triggers is key to dismantling them.

Procrastination

First, fear doesn't vanish entirely; it can morph into perfectionism. Felix overcame his crippling anxiety from the first life, but vestiges remain in the form of wanting to do things flawlessly. If he cannot guarantee success, he reasons that waiting might improve his odds. This logic, while seemingly harmless, traps him in a cycle of hoping for the perfect time. Each passing day convinces him that better circumstances might appear tomorrow.

Second, Felix remembers how the second life lulled him into comfort. Now, he dreads repeating that mistake, so he becomes overly cautious about committing to a plan. You might see a similar pattern in your life: the more you fear slipping back into old habits, the harder it can be to take meaningful steps, in case you pick the wrong approach. In Felix's mind, any step that could echo his previous complacency must be avoided or delayed until he is certain it's a worthwhile move. This paradoxically results in prolonged inaction.

Third, there is a sense of endless time. Felix believes he has multiple lives ahead, indeed, he's only on his third, and the memory of having died and come back fosters the illusion that tomorrow is guaranteed. Whenever the pressure to act arises, he pushes it aside, telling himself that he is young in this particular life. This mindset mirrors how people postpone critical tasks, assuming they have "plenty of years left" to do them. That assumption can be dangerously misleading.

Fourth, Felix's environment offers distractions aplenty. When you have no pressing threat or immediate scarcity, you can easily fill your time with minor pleasures. A soft sunlit patch, a friendly human offering a treat, the chance to simply lounge in a safe corner, none of these are wrong, but they can become persistent detours when you consistently pick them over the tasks that truly matter. Without external urgency, procrastination finds fertile ground.

Fifth, there is an emotional component to procrastination. Felix sometimes senses that tackling a goal might involve discomfort or effort. Maybe he wants to explore a tricky rooftop or develop alliances that require awkward introductions. Those steps demand energy and risk. To avoid that discomfort, he convinces himself that there is no immediate rush. Similarly, you might dodge that phone call or that big project because of the tension it stirs inside, telling yourself you will be braver or more ready later.

These root causes often intersect. One day, Felix might procrastinate because he idealises perfect conditions. The next, he might avoid a task because he doesn't feel mentally prepared. Over time, these justifications stack up. He forms a habit of always finding a reason not to do the most important things. Even though each excuse may hold a seed of truth, together they build a barrier separating him from genuine progress.

It's crucial to remember that procrastination doesn't always stem from laziness. Felix is not lazy in the traditional sense. He still hunts occasionally, interacts with other cats, and moves around. The trouble is that he never tackles the more significant ventures, like forging new territories or thoroughly improving his skills, because those are the tasks that require deliberate effort and potential vulnerability. Subconsciously, Felix believes if he delays these bigger actions, he avoids confronting the possibility of failure or discomfort.

You might see how this pattern forms in your own day-to-day routines. Rather than making a difficult decision, you focus on easy chores. Instead of diving into a challenging assignment, you do quick tasks that deliver instant satisfaction. This approach shields you from the fear of not performing well, but it also prevents you from ever reaching a deeper level of accomplishment. Procrastination becomes a self-protective mechanism, blocking disappointment at the expense of progress.

Overcoming these causes requires honest introspection. Felix would need to admit that he is still partly afraid of failing, even if fear no longer rules him like it did in his first life. He might also need to accept that perfect conditions rarely exist and that a decent start now is usually better than a perfect start never. Recognising how fleeting each life can be might spur him to make the most of his days, rather than acting as though he has infinite tomorrows.

Yet these insights don't come easily. Many of the root causes lurk beneath the surface, shaped by Felix's memories and instincts. He might sense something is off but struggle to pinpoint the exact reason. Without clarity, the habit of delay grows stronger, each day reinforcing the notion that postponing tasks is normal and inconsequential.

In the sections that follow, you will see how these root causes play out in Felix's life. Procrastination starts to nibble away at his chances, much like a mouse in a forgotten pantry. By the time he notices the extent of the damage, he may have too little time left to fix it. As with the previous lives, the real question is whether Felix will break free from these patterns in time to salvage any part of his third life or whether he will once again reach the end, wishing he had acted sooner.

Procrastination's Impact on Potential

Imagine a day where Felix wakes up brimming with ideas. Perhaps he has a plan to claim a new rooftop lookout, confident that it will provide both safety and a perfect vantage for hunting. Yet, rather than setting out immediately, he finds a dozen small distractions. He lounges in a sunny spot, eyes half-closed, telling himself he will climb the rooftop later. Afternoon comes, and he is sidetracked by a passing cat. Evening arrives, and he decides it's too dark to attempt something risky. By bedtime, the day is gone, and he's made no progress. This is how procrastination quietly shrinks a cat's potential.

You might think of moments in your own life where you intended to do something that mattered, writing that book, pursuing a new job, or reaching out to an old friend, but ended up letting the day slip by. The cost is not just the missed goal; it's the subtle erosion of your belief in what you could achieve. Each time you fail to act, you reinforce a narrative that important tasks can always be deferred. Before long, you doubt your ability to follow through at all.

In Felix's case, the habit of delay robs him of confidence. He realises, on some level, that although he yearns to do more, he seldom does. Gradually, his self-image suffers. He becomes a cat with big ideas and minimal action, living in a cycle of half-promises. The more he sees this pattern repeat, the less he trusts himself to seize any opportunities when they arise.

Procrastination also stifles exploration. In earlier lives, fear or comfort might have stopped Felix from venturing out. Now, ironically, it's the perpetual "I'll do it tomorrow" that bars him from new experiences. Each passing day, he puts off investigating that orchard or forging a better alliance, other cats step in and claim those resources. By the time Felix finally stirs, prime spots are occupied, or the chance to gain an advantage is lost.

One tragedy of procrastination is how it can cloud your awareness of time. Because you always plan to do things "later," you barely notice the weeks accelerating. In your mind, you still see the opportunities as open. Felix might say to himself, "That rooftop will be there tomorrow," ignoring the fact that a stronger cat might claim it in the meantime. Or the roof might become inaccessible if a homeowner blocks it off. In real life, you might postpone a skill until you have "spare time," only to look back years later and see you never found that time.

Another harmful effect is that procrastination leads to shallow engagement. Since Felix rarely follows through, he drifts in a sort of indecisive haze. He never becomes deeply invested in one project or relationship, always telling himself he can pick it up in the future if he wants. Consequently, he floats on the surface of life, never diving into the depths where true growth happens. You might know this feeling if you keep dabbling in tasks without committing to any, ending up with little expertise or satisfaction.

In a broader sense, procrastination also strains social bonds. If Felix keeps telling other cats, "Yes, let's explore tomorrow," only to bail out each time, they lose trust in him. His reputation suffers, and he misses out on team efforts that require reliability. Over time, they stop inviting him, convinced he will only delay or come up with excuses. Thus, he loses not only the chance to expand his territory but also the camaraderie that could enrich his life.

The cost to Felix's well-being also rises. Deep inside, he feels unsettled, sensing that he is not living up to his potential. That quiet tension grows, feeding a background unease. Yet, ironically, stress can make him procrastinate further. He might think, "I'm too anxious today; I should rest until I feel better." This cycle can lock him into an endless loop of inaction, fueled by the discomfort of knowing he is squandering opportunities.

Over time, procrastination can spawn genuine regret. If you look back on a week of missed chances, you might shrug it off. Look back on a lifetime, and the picture becomes painful. This is the difference between minor delays and a deep-seated pattern of avoidance. Felix doesn't see the final shape of his third life yet, but you, as the observer, can sense the gathering storm. Each day of deferral moves him closer to the point where redemption might be out of reach.

A final, often overlooked, impact is that procrastination blinds you to urgent needs. Suppose a certain section of the neighbourhood is becoming too dangerous or a new group of hostile cats is moving in. If Felix delays investigating or forging alliances, he could be caught off guard. By the time he realises the severity of the threat, it could be too late to adapt effectively. Life rarely remains static, so hesitating can magnify problems you might have nipped in the bud if you'd acted promptly.

This chapter in Felix's saga reveals how procrastination slowly saps his sense of purpose, community, and self-trust. Much like fear and comfort, it appears benign initially, even appealing in its promise of "plenty of time." Yet, it gradually strangles the possibility of living fully in the here and now. As you continue, you will see how philosophical insights might help Felix (and you) grasp the subtle dangers of delaying what matters and how each life we have is too short to spend dreaming about "later."

Philosophical Insights on Procrastination

Throughout history, many thinkers have probed the nature of procrastination. You might recall that in his second life, Felix explored how philosophers addressed fear and comfort. Now, he encounters ideas about delay and how it thwarts a meaningful life. Even as a cat, certain reflections resonate with him, offering guidance on breaking the cycle of "I'll do it tomorrow."

One enduring perspective is that humans and, by analogy, cats like Felix undervalue the present moment. Philosophers have pointed out that the future is uncertain, and putting tasks off assumes you will have the same health, resources, or motivation at a later date. In ancient Stoic thought, focusing on what you can do now is a key virtue. Marcus Aurelius wrote about the fleeting nature of life, stressing the need to seize each day. Felix doesn't read texts, but if he did, he might find a warning: delay is a gambler's habit, betting on tomorrow without knowing if tomorrow will come.

Existential philosophy adds another angle. By endlessly putting off decisions, you avoid the responsibility of shaping your life. You remain in a state of indecision, refusing to define your essence through action. For Felix, that means he never truly commits to exploring, building alliances, or accomplishing feats. He lives in a grey area of possibility rather than the vivid realm of doing. While this feels safe, it also leaves him with no real identity or sense of achievement.

Meanwhile, practical wisdom emphasises that small steps taken immediately often yield more progress than large, idealised plans postponed indefinitely. Many spiritual teachers echo this sentiment, encouraging daily discipline over waiting for inspired bursts. If Felix applied this, he might say, "I'll check out half the orchard today and the other half tomorrow," rather than waiting for the perfect day to do it all. By taking incremental actions, he would at least begin the journey, gathering momentum that counters procrastination's stall.

Mindfulness teaches that part of procrastination's power lies in letting the mind wander to future scenarios, focusing on what might go wrong or how you might feel more ready later. By grounding yourself in the present, you notice that the tasks you fear are often manageable when tackled one moment at a time. Felix might find that simply hopping onto a low wall is not hard, so maybe the next jump onto a higher fence is also feasible. Each present-moment choice chips away at the illusion that everything must happen in one perfect move.

Philosophers have also argued that procrastination can signal deeper emotional needs. Perhaps you postpone a goal because you secretly fear what success might demand of you or worry it could change your relationships. Felix might sense that exploring the orchard could bring new responsibilities or lead him into conflicts he feels unprepared for. Rather than confront that possibility, he pushes it aside. Being honest with himself about these inner reservations could help him see that procrastination is masking deeper anxieties.

There's also a strong link between procrastination and mortality. Reflecting on life's fragility, as the Stoics recommended, can spur you to act. If Felix truly appreciated that each life can end, sometimes abruptly, he might feel compelled to use his third life right away. He has, after all, already lost two lives and should know better than to assume an endless string of tomorrows. Yet memory is fuzzy, and the illusion of time lures him back to delay. Philosophical teachings urge you to remember that tomorrow is never guaranteed, making now a precious resource.

An intriguing angle is that procrastination can impede ethical growth. By putting off tasks, you also defer helping others or contributing to your community. Felix, in his drifting state, misses chances to assist fellow cats or to form alliances that could benefit the entire block. His inaction isn't just personal neglect; it might deny others the support or camaraderie he could provide. Ethically, then, procrastination hinders the good you could do in the world.

Finally, many philosophical schools advocate the virtue of resolve, cultivating a mindset that once you decide something is important, you follow through despite fluctuating moods or uncertain conditions. Felix wavers day by day, letting minor inconveniences stop him. A more resolute approach would see him forging ahead even if he feels a bit tired or the weather is not perfect. This quality of steadfastness separates fleeting wishes from genuine commitments.

The main takeaway for Felix, and for you, is that procrastination is not a trivial flaw; it's an existential problem that shapes who you become. Every time you delay, you let life slip through your claws. Philosophical reflections, whether stoic, existential, or mindful, all converge on a single imperative: do not waste this fleeting window. If Felix grasps these ideas, he might shift his behaviour before the final dawn of his third life arrives. If not, he risks another exit marked by remorse, having once again discovered truth too late.

Breaking the Cycle of Delay

Armed with a vague sense that procrastination is robbing him, Felix begins looking for solutions. He has neither the immediate crisis that once forced him to confront fear nor the slow suffocation of comfort pressing on him. Yet a gnawing feeling builds, telling him that he cannot keep postponing important steps. If you have felt that subtle anxiety, you know it can be a catalyst for change or a reason to procrastinate more. The outcome depends on your choices.

First, Felix decides to set simple, immediate goals. Rather than telling himself, "I'll explore the entire orchard sometime soon," he picks a specific day, tomorrow at sunrise, and promises to check at least one corner of it. He shares this plan with another cat, Sable, who agrees to meet him there. By creating a tiny but concrete appointment, Felix reduces his freedom to delay. This method mirrors a well-known tactic: turn vague intentions into clear commitments backed by a deadline or a partner who keeps you accountable.

He also embraces the notion of incremental progress. When morning comes, Felix is tempted to sleep in. His mind drifts to the idea that a slightly sunnier day would be better for orchard exploration. But then he recalls his vow to Sable. Rather than exploring the whole orchard, he decides he can at least take a peek at the fence line. This partial success emboldens him. Once he arrives, curiosity nibbles away at further hesitation, and he ends up exploring more than planned. That's the power of starting small: once you're in motion, it feels easier to continue.

Another strategy he adopts is to tackle tasks before diving into distractions. He used to lounge in a sunlit patch immediately after waking, telling himself he would begin exploring later. Now, he flips the sequence: a quick check of the orchard first, then a relaxed nap if time allows. By taking action early, he avoids letting the day drift away in trivial comforts. In your case, this might mean you do the toughest chore first thing, so the sense of achievement propels the rest of your day.

Mindfulness also helps. Each time Felix catches himself thinking, "I'll do it later," he tries to pause and question that impulse. Is there a genuine reason for delay, or is it just the usual excuse? Sometimes, genuine fatigue or external threats might justify waiting. But often, it's a habit of pushing tasks onto the imaginary future. By becoming aware of this reflex, Felix gains the power to disrupt it. You might do the same in your life: when you catch yourself saying, "Later," ask if this is a protective strategy or a genuine need.

Felix's plan also includes rewarding himself for taking action. After exploring a new sector of the orchard or forging a brief alliance with a neighbouring cat, he allows himself a treat, perhaps a cosy nap or a playful chase of a fluttering leaf. This positive reinforcement helps him associate progress with satisfaction. Instead of always rewarding rest and comfort first, he earns them through effort, striking a healthier balance between enjoyment and productivity.

Step by step, Felix realises that procrastination is less about lacking time and more about lacking commitment. Once he commits to small tasks every day, his progress accelerates. He regains a sense of control, no longer drifting in an ocean of vague intentions. This boost in self-trust unlocks further motivation, prompting him to see how much he squandered earlier in his third life. Though he cannot recover those lost days, he can make the best of what remains.

However, old habits die hard. Now and then, Felix catches himself slipping, telling Sable he will join her on a hunt "perhaps tomorrow." The difference is that he notices this moment of delay and corrects himself before it becomes a pattern. That awareness, gleaned from mindful practice, helps him break the cycle. He might slip up once or twice, but he no longer spirals into endless postponement.

Crucially, Felix also learns the value of deadlines. In the past, he never set time frames for his goals, letting them float indefinitely. Now, if he wants to climb a certain rooftop, he vows to attempt it by the end of the week. If he intends to befriend a certain group of cats, he arranges a meeting within days. These self-imposed limits bring a sense of urgency that counters his natural inclination to wait. You might do the same with personal or professional targets, understanding that open-ended tasks often fall to the bottom of your priority list.

Additionally, Felix starts confiding in cats who can help. He admits to Sable that he has a habit of pushing things off. By airing that truth, he feels more accountable. Sable occasionally nudges him, meowing pointedly, "Weren't you supposed to check the orchard's north edge today?" Though this can be uncomfortable, it is the discomfort Felix needs to keep moving.

Over time, these strategies begin to crack the shell of procrastination. Felix experiences the exhilaration of actual accomplishment. He finds vantage points with better hunts, discovers new allies, and shapes a more dynamic existence. Each success cements the idea that doing something now is far more valuable than dreaming about it for tomorrow. Yet the ultimate question remains: will this realisation come soon enough to fully redeem his third life, or is Felix once again on borrowed time?

Conclusion of Third Life

Felix's third life unfolds in the flicker between determination and delay. He never again cowers in fear or sinks into idle comfort, but he faces the subtle tyranny of postponement. "I'll do it later", weaves through his days, stealing the energy of now. Only when he finally senses the cost of endless delaying does he act, stepping into small commitments, mindful checks, and clearer deadlines. For a while, it seems he might overturn this procrastinating fate, seizing the potential so often talked about but seldom claimed.

Yet, as with his earlier lives, Felix's window of opportunity has a limit. After delaying for too long, time accelerates. The orchard he had hoped to explore fully is half-seen; the alliances he planned to deepen remain tentative. Though he tries to recover, his body again shows signs of ageing, and the environment shifts in ways he can't fully predict. The unstoppable cycle of nature, combined with lingering bouts of procrastination, closes in. In the end, Felix realises he has only partly lived out this life's promise.

The 9th Life of Felix The Cat

He passes from this world with a bittersweet knowledge: delaying matters can rob you of the one thing you can never replenish: time. As his third life fades, Felix clings to the understanding that tomorrow is never as certain or as perfect as one imagines. Though regret traces his final breaths, a spark of hope remains. The lessons he gathered, however late, will echo in the next life. Perhaps, at last, he will learn to act decisively with no illusions of waiting. You, witnessing his slow dance with procrastination, can take heed. Do what must be done while you have the strength to do it, for the line between one life and the next is thinner than any cat could ever predict.

The Fourth Life

Seeking Approval

You have watched Felix struggle with three stumbling blocks so far: paralysing fear in his first life, the lull of comfort in his second, and the slow drain of procrastination in his third. Each time, Felix left that life with crucial lessons he only fully grasped at the final moment. Now, in his fourth existence, Felix longs to apply what he has learned. He wants to be brave, active, and efficient with his precious days.

Yet a new snare lurks one that slithers subtly into his thoughts and nudges him to live for others. This time, Felix craves approval above all. He grows convinced that he must please every cat he meets, hoping to gain admiration and acceptance. While that might sound harmless, it quickly morphs into a desperate chase for validation. Felix becomes so focused on how others perceive him that he forgets his genuine goals and desires.

This chapter follows Felix as he navigates the tricky terrain of seeking constant endorsement. He thinks he is simply being friendly and cooperative, but in truth, he is bending and twisting his nature to match external expectations. Through five subheadings, you will see how the need for approval sneaks into decisions, how it shapes Felix's sense of worth, the ways it reduces his freedom, the philosophical insights that question such a life, and the steps required to break this unfulfilling cycle. By the end, you will wonder if Felix can change course before his fourth life runs out. The pursuit of approval might appear less damaging than raw fear or overwhelming comfort, but it can still strip you of authenticity and leave you empty-handed at the end of each day.

The Trap of External Validation

In this new life, Felix wakes feeling confident that he will not repeat his old mistakes. He is neither trembling at every rustle nor lazing in endless rest. He is also aware of how time can slip away if he delays important actions. One might think he is well set for a purposeful existence, ready to accomplish things he postponed or never dared attempt. Yet, as soon as Felix begins exploring, an unexpected craving takes hold: he wants to be liked by every cat he meets.

At first, this urge feels normal. After all, social acceptance can help you find protection, companionship, and shared resources. Felix notices that if he behaves politely and echoes the opinions of the cats around him, he receives purrs of approval and friendly tail twitches. Encouraged by these responses, Felix starts adapting his entire demeanour to please others. Whenever he encounters a confident cat, he pretends he is equally bold and adventurous, even if his mood is quiet that day. If he meets a timid cat, he acts demure, sensing it will soothe the other's nerves.

You might see how easy it is to slip into such patterns in your own circles. Being agreeable often leads to smoother interactions, so you lean into it. Yet the more you do, the more you risk losing the essence of who you are. Felix begins to notice that he no longer trusts his instincts. Before he speaks, or meows, in his case, he wonders, "Will this be liked? Will they approve?" Instead of following his real preferences, Felix picks whichever stance he thinks will earn him the most praise in the moment.

Seeking Approval

This habit soon becomes a trap. Whenever two groups of cats hold conflicting views, Felix tries to appease both, contorting himself so neither side feels offended. He denies his own opinions and feelings to maintain a fleeting sense of harmony. The result is a shallow kind of popularity: plenty of cats regard Felix as pleasant, but few truly know him. Felix, meanwhile, grows restless because he never expresses his honest thoughts. He has replaced self-discovery with a mask, hoping it will keep him universally loved.

It gets worse when Felix encounters cats who thrive on attention. They praise him one day, then tease him the next, watching how he reacts. Because Felix so desperately wants their approval, he adjusts himself even further. He might adopt a mannerism he dislikes or agree to tasks that do not suit him, all in the hope of winning favour again. It is never enough. The same cats who compliment him for certain traits mock him when he fails to live up to their demands. Felix responds by pushing himself harder to meet their mercurial standards.

You might recognise this scenario if you have ever found yourself trapped in the opinions of others, bending your choices and identity to earn praise. Seeking validation can feel good short term, like a quick rush when someone nods in admiration. Over time, though, it hollows you out. You may no longer act on what resonates with your true self, but on what you predict will gain applause. The tragedy is that even if you succeed in pleasing everyone, you might lose the satisfaction of acting with authenticity.

The trap of external validation also affects Felix's plans. Suppose he wants to climb a certain wall or investigate a new area. If a popular cat scoffs at his ambition, Felix backtracks and pretends he never wanted it. If others fawn over a different route or hobby, he mirrors their enthusiasm, telling himself it might be better to follow the crowd. This chameleon-like approach robs Felix of direction. Rather than forging a path that challenges or excites him, he always looks over his shoulder, worried about how others judge his steps.

Another problem with external validation is that it often depends on short-lived impressions. A cat might compliment Felix for being adventurous one day, but if he shows caution the next, that same cat might belittle him. Chasing approval becomes like chasing a moving target. Felix invests energy in maintaining the right image, yet the criteria shift constantly. Meanwhile, he makes no real progress in personal goals or deeper connections.

Eventually, Felix notices an emptiness inside. Although he garners casual admiration, he does not feel truly respected, because he never takes a genuine stand. He realises that his so-called friendships lack substance, since he only presents whatever version of himself others expect. The fleeting nature of this praise leaves him anxious, craving more affirmation, yet never feeling secure. The trap has sprung: each dose of external approval soothes him momentarily, while fuelling a deeper insecurity that he cannot be loved for his authentic self.

In your own life, you might see how easy it is to end up in this cycle. You start by trying to be amicable, thinking it will help you integrate into a group or avoid conflict. Soon, you measure your worth by the smiles and nods you receive. If they vanish, you panic and do more to regain them. Before you know it, you do not even recall your own opinions or style.

Like Felix, you have become a mirror reflecting others, hoping they will shine approval back at you.

Thus, in his fourth life, Felix drifts into a new kind of captivity. Rather than cowering in fear, dozing in comfort, or putting everything off, he devotes himself to pleasing the crowd. He cannot see the full damage yet, but the early signs are there: a loss of genuine direction and a creeping sense of inauthenticity. It is a gentle trap, but one that can be just as confining as the most rigid cage. The question is whether Felix will recognise the bars in time to set himself free.

Why We Crave Acceptance

You might wonder what drives Felix to chase approval so eagerly. After all, he has lived through three previous existences, each teaching him the value of self-awareness and purposeful action. Yet, beneath these lessons lie more primal urges. Part of every being's nature, feline or human, is the wish to belong. This need can be helpful, forging communities and mutual support, but it can also become a compulsion that overshadows personal integrity.

In Felix's mind, a few factors intertwine to make him vulnerable to this craving. First, his memory of fear still lingers. He recalls how, in his first life, loneliness and tension suffocated him. If no one stood by his side, he felt at risk. Having discovered the benefit of companionship in life two and three, he now associates approval with safety. He thinks that if enough cats like him, he will never face a threat alone.

Second, Felix is aware of how procrastination once robbed him of success. He wants to avoid that kind of idle drifting. In his mind, pleasing others becomes a quick way to show he is active and engaged. If he can prove his sociability, he convinces himself that he is not wasting time. He interprets positive feedback from others as a sign of productivity, even though he might be ignoring tasks that matter most to him.

Third, Felix underestimates the subtlety of genuine connections. He believes that if he can just gather a large circle of cats who smile at him, it means he is forging strong bonds. The truth is that real friendship often includes conflict, differences of opinion, and the need to stand firm. By trying to keep everything smooth and agreeable, Felix might accumulate more acquaintances but fewer authentic supporters who truly understand him.

Biologically, social animals like cats are wired to value group acceptance to some extent. Stray felines often cluster for warmth or survival. This innate drive to not be rejected can expand into an overdeveloped desire for external validation. You might notice a similar push in yourself when you join a new workplace or social group. Initially, you want to be accepted, but that need can spiral into an obsession if left unchecked.

Another root cause is insecurity. Having endured fear, comfort, and procrastination, Felix may feel uncertain about his true capabilities. Seeking approval from others becomes a shortcut to feeling worthy. Each nod or purr of satisfaction from a peer bolsters his sense of self. Yet it is a shaky foundation. If the applause stops, Felix's confidence crumbles, since he has tied his worth to their fleeting opinions.

In your own life, chasing approval might also stem from a childhood or early lesson where acceptance was conditional. Perhaps you learned that making others happy guaranteed you would be liked, so you repeated that behaviour. Over time, it solidified into an identity that depends on outside feedback. Felix undergoes a version of this. As he meets more cats, he feels each new encounter demands perfect performance to secure acceptance. The cycle of pleasing others quickly becomes automatic.

Cultural norms, in a feline sense, can shape this drive too. If local cats idolise a certain style, Felix might adopt it, fearing he will be seen as backward or outcast if he does not. He starts wearing himself thin trying to keep up with every new preference that emerges. This frantic effort leaves him exhausted, yet he cannot stop, since rejection feels like an existential threat. You might recall how, in fear or comfort, Felix was pinned down by circumstance. Now, ironically, he is pinned down by social pressure.

A deeper psychological layer is the notion of identity confusion. If you are not secure in who you are, you allow others' opinions to guide you. Felix has some partial memories of the goals he once held dear, but he has not fully reflected on them. The moment he realises a group disapproves, he abandons those goals, thinking, "Maybe that idea was foolish." Without a strong inner compass, external approval becomes his only marker of direction.

Yet, as you will see, living for others' praise carries a hefty price. Felix is about to discover that bending to every whim leaves him directionless and fatigued. Each time he tries to please one group, another group offers contrasting demands. Pleasing both is impossible. This push-and-pull dynamic forms a tangled net, capturing Felix's every choice. Rather than building a stable sense of community, he ends up scattered, with no deep alliances or personal pride in his decisions.

The seeds of discomfort begin to sprout. Felix, though initially gratified by the friendly mews and purrs, starts to feel hollow. Some cats sense that he never truly contradicts anyone, so they doubt his sincerity. A few even begin to tease him, testing how far he will go to maintain acceptance. Facing this subtle bullying, Felix feels helpless. He cannot stand up for himself without risking disapproval, which he dreads more than anything else. So, he yields, or tries to appease, and further loses his sense of self.

This points to the core reason we sometimes crave acceptance so fiercely: a fear of standing alone. We worry that if we contradict the group, we will be cast out, left vulnerable. Yet real belonging often involves disagreements, self-assertion, and mutual respect. Felix, believing that unconditional agreement is the key to popularity, misses the chance for genuine connection. His craving for acceptance, while natural in small doses, has grown into a force that rules him.

By exploring these root causes, you see that Felix's path in the fourth life is shaped by both his old anxieties and new misunderstandings. If he cannot tackle them, he will remain caught in a chase that never satisfies. Perhaps you notice elements of your own life here, moments when you compromised your beliefs for approval, or shaped your identity around others' expectations. It is a universal struggle, and one Felix will need to face sooner rather than later if he wants his fourth life to be more than another half-lived chapter.

The Cost of Living for Approval

Seeking Approval

Following a few weeks of careful observation, you might think Felix's social success is impressive. He is on good terms with several neighbourhood cats, who recognise him as the affable one who rarely ruffles fur. He flits among them, meowing amiably and never contradicting any viewpoint too strongly. If you asked the local felines, they might say Felix is pleasant and easy to get along with. On the surface, it seems he has found a positive niche.

Yet behind the scenes, Felix feels a gnawing sense of dissatisfaction. Yes, he is gathering compliments, but he senses a lack of true closeness. He jumps from group to group, tailoring his behaviour to whatever standard they uphold. One group praises bold hunts, another reveres quiet introspection, and Felix tries to do both, often in the same day. This constant shape-shifting leaves him mentally exhausted. He rarely engages in solitary reflection, since any moment spent alone feels like a risk: if he is not present to adapt, maybe the others will forget him.

In practical terms, living for approval forces Felix to neglect personal growth. He does not dare attempt certain challenges unless they are guaranteed to earn applause. If some cats believe scaling a high fence is reckless, Felix hesitates, worried they will disapprove if he attempts it. If others think rummaging through bins is beneath them, he avoids that too, even if it might be beneficial. Over time, his capacity for taking initiative atrophies. He becomes a follower, scanning the crowd to see which action will make him look best.

Another cost is that Felix loses creative thinking. Rather than exploring his own ideas or unique methods, he constantly imitates what he thinks others favour. This stifles innovation.

He might have discovered a clever shortcut across rooftops, but if no one else is interested, he tosses the idea aside. You may have felt that discouragement as well, an exciting concept you suppress because the group around you disdains it or finds it odd.

This pattern sabotages deeper relationships too. True friendship requires honesty and the willingness to share differing points of view. By always agreeing, Felix denies others the chance to know the real him. In private moments, certain cats might suspect Felix is hiding something or faking his enthusiasm. Trust begins to waver. The more he tries to hold onto universal approval, the less he convinces anyone that he is genuine. It is a subtle irony: in hoping to please everyone, he inspires doubt rather than admiration.

Additionally, the chase for validation breeds anxiety. Felix cannot relax, because acceptance can shift like the wind. A cat who once admired his calm demeanour might criticise him tomorrow for not being bold. Another cat who liked his playful side might reject him if he fails to entertain them next time. By anchoring his sense of security in other cats' ever-changing opinions, Felix spins in a loop of constant worry about how he is perceived.

Beyond emotional strain, the social costs mount. If a conflict arises between two groups, Felix faces a dilemma. Whose side does he take? He tries to placate both, resulting in accusations that he is disloyal or indecisive. Soon, he becomes a target for blame, since each side notices he is not truly committed. The veneer of affability might get him through mild disagreements, but serious rifts expose his lack of convictions.

Seeking Approval

You also see the diminishing returns of such a strategy. Early on, cats appreciate Felix's pleasant manner. Over time, though, they take his compliance for granted. They expect him to do whatever they want, losing respect for his opinions. The more he yields, the less they see him as an equal. Instead, he is relegated to the role of a sycophant who simply echoes the loudest voice. In your world, you might have noticed similar patterns: a people-pleaser can be liked initially but is seldom truly respected.

Felix's inner life suffers most of all. He occasionally recalls moments from his previous lives where he acted with some measure of authenticity. Even in fear or comfort, he had glimpses of his own desires. Now, that self has become murky. He wonders what he actually likes, beyond the fleeting praise of the crowd. The sad truth is that he cannot recall. Every choice is shaped by external input. This hollowing out of identity weighs on him, although he struggles to name it.

Eventually, the cost extends to missed opportunities. A cat named Rowan, who once admired Felix's potential, invites him to join a venture exploring distant rooftops. Felix agrees initially, wanting Rowan's approval, but then he learns that some influential cats ridicule the idea as "pointless wandering." Desperate to keep their favour, Felix pretends he never intended to go. Rowan, disappointed, stops reaching out. Over time, these lost chances accumulate. Felix's day-to-day life remains bland, as he invests his efforts in groupthink rather than self-directed growth.

This is how living for approval drains your future. Each time you compromise for the sake of applause, you discard a fragment of who you might have become. You also risk losing alliances with those who would prefer you stand firm. Felix does not see the full scale of the damage yet, but the cracks are forming. He is superficially popular, but deeply unfulfilled. You might have encountered situations in your own journey where you said "yes" to someone else's idea simply to be liked, even though your gut pulled in another direction. In small doses, it might be harmless, but as a life-long pattern, it can leave you regretful and directionless.

Thus, the price of living for approval emerges in many forms: lost individuality, strained trust, shallow relationships, and a perpetual sense of insecurity. By now, Felix feels something is off, but he cannot break the cycle without a profound shift in how he views acceptance. The coming sections explore whether he can glean wisdom from philosophical reflections, something that has helped him before, and whether he can pivot before another life ends in dissatisfaction.

Philosophical Insights on Authenticity

In earlier lives, Felix discovered that philosophical thought can illuminate the hidden traps shaping his behaviour. Now, as he flounders in the sea of approval, these teachings become more vital than ever. If he can reflect on them, he might understand why living for outside endorsement is doomed to fail, and why forging a grounded sense of self is crucial.

A recurring theme across many philosophical schools is the importance of being true to your nature. Stoics, for instance, suggest that external events, including others' opinions, lie beyond your full control. Marcus Aurelius urged people to focus on their own virtues and duties rather than seeking applause. Translating this into feline terms, Felix might see that the shifting moods of the local cats are not his to manage. He can only direct his intentions and actions. If he obsesses over controlling their approval, he will never find peace.

Existential thinkers emphasise personal responsibility and authenticity. By conforming to whatever the crowd wants, Felix loses his essence. In existential thought, you create meaning by choosing your path, even if it differs from the majority. If Felix always checks whether others approve, he forfeits the power to define himself. This caution might shield him from short-term conflict, but it robs him of deeper purpose and identity.

Meanwhile, Eastern philosophies such as Zen highlight the danger of clinging to external attachments, including praise. By craving approval, Felix places his self-worth in the hands of external forces. Zen wisdom would advise him to act from a place of calm awareness, free from the push and pull of social desires. The cat who moves in harmony with his inner sense of right action, rather than external signals, can remain centred even when others criticise or misunderstand him.

If Felix were to integrate these ideas, he would need to accept that not everyone will always applaud. This might be the scariest realisation for him. He must also accept that conflict or disapproval are normal parts of standing firm. Authentic living does not require rudeness or aggression, but it does mean you refuse to lie about your thoughts just to secure a pat on the back. Fearful of rejection, Felix must learn that a genuine friend respects honesty, even if it stings occasionally.

Another angle is the notion that constant approval-seeking feeds ego rather than fostering genuine harmony. Philosophers caution that the ego craves recognition but struggles to handle rejection. When you are entangled in your ego, you take every negative comment personally and mistake every compliment as proof of worth. Felix, tumbling in the highs and lows of other cats' opinions, never establishes an independent sense of self. He might find, if he steps away from the egoic chase, that his life gains stability as he acts in line with his personal convictions.

Mindfulness-based teachings also suggest that focusing too heavily on external applause distracts you from the present moment. Felix is always scanning the environment to see how others respond, which prevents him from noticing what is actually happening in his own mind or physical surroundings. If he slowed down and paid attention to what he truly feels, he might spot the tension that arises when he fakes agreement. Recognising that discomfort could guide him toward more sincere choices, even if they risk short-term disapproval.

Philosophical thought thus challenges the assumption that universal popularity leads to happiness. In fact, many great thinkers argue that a dash of solitude, conflict, or opposition can strengthen character. A cat who dares to follow a unique path might face scorn, but also experiences genuine achievements and relationships rooted in respect. Felix, if he embraced this idea, would no longer define success by how many cats purr at him, but by how many honest connections he maintains while honouring his inner voice.

Combining these teachings, Felix could begin a path to authenticity. He might practise telling the truth gently when he disagrees, or trying a bold action even if the crowd might mock him. Such steps would be risky, but they offer a route out of the emptiness of constant approval-seeking. By adopting a philosophy of inward alignment rather than outward flattery, he could reclaim ownership of his decisions.

However, integrating these lessons requires courage. Felix cannot simply read a proverb and be cured. He must live them through real encounters, risking immediate criticism to forge deeper integrity. If he does so, he might discover that some cats appreciate his honesty more than his flattery, while others drift away, resentful that he no longer panders to them. The net result, though, is a more stable sense of self and a circle of relationships based on mutual respect rather than hollow applause.

This philosophical awakening might also remind Felix that time is finite. Each day spent faking an identity is a day not used to explore genuine potential. Some schools of thought underscore how each mortal being has an unknown expiry. For Felix, who has glimpsed his own mortality multiple times, this should resonate. If he truly accepts that his fourth life, like the ones before it, can end at any moment, the urgency to live truthfully intensifies. Approval becomes less alluring than the precious chance to be himself.

As he wades through these insights, Felix stands on the threshold between illusions of popularity and the reality of authenticity. Philosophical wisdom lights a path, but the choice to walk it belongs to him alone. If he embraces it, he might salvage this life before it slips away. If he clings to the comfort of universal approval, he may once again confront regret at the final breath, realising he traded authenticity for applause that vanished when he needed it most.

Breaking Free from the Need for Approval

Armed with an emerging awareness, Felix starts to question his obsession with applause. He notices how often he asks himself, "What will they think?" rather than, "What do I think?" This shift in perspective is subtle but critical. It suggests Felix is ready to challenge the need for constant approval. Yet knowing a problem exists is only the beginning. He must learn concrete steps to reclaim his independence.

His first tactic is to practise small acts of honesty. When a group of cats chat about a new hunting method, Felix dares to express a different view if he genuinely disagrees. Even though his heart pounds, worried they might sneer, he forces himself to speak frankly. Sometimes, a cat wrinkles its nose, but occasionally another cat nods, intrigued. Felix discovers that not every disagreement leads to punishment. This encourages him to keep being honest, realising that authenticity can foster genuine interest rather than hostility.

Next, Felix tries spending more time alone, despite his lingering fear of missing out on social recognition. Finding a quiet spot near an abandoned garden, he reflects on his personal goals. He realises he has always wanted to scale a particular rooftop, even though certain cats call it dangerous. A spark of excitement ignites, tempered by the memory of how he once suppressed that urge for approval's sake. This time, Felix decides to follow his own instinct, telling only a close friend, Rowan, who supports him without judgment.

The climb is not easy. Felix's limbs tremble halfway up, and a part of him wonders if the critics were right. Yet he also feels invigorated. Something inside him, something that does not care about external applause, pushes him to continue. When he finally reaches the top, the view is astonishing. He sees the rooftops stretching far into the distance, alive with possibilities he never imagined from ground level. In that moment, he tastes the thrill of living for his own reasons rather than for a pat on the back. The sense of accomplishment does not vanish when he realises no one else is there to cheer him on; it deepens, powered by self-respect.

This experience spurs Felix to set personal milestones. He jots them down mentally, reminding himself that each target is for his satisfaction, not a performance for the crowd. You might adopt a similar approach, listing your genuine aims and tracking them in private. By removing the need for public praise, you learn to gauge success through your own lens. Each goal completed cements your sense of identity, independent of popular opinion.

Felix also learns to handle criticism with composure. When he returns from the rooftop, a few cats scoff, calling him a show-off. Instead of scrambling to please them, Felix calmly explains that he did it for his own curiosity, not to impress anyone. This honesty disrupts their attempt to shame him. Some cats remain unimpressed, but Felix realises their opinions no longer control his feelings. He has anchored his contentment in an experience that was personally meaningful, so outside negativity carries less weight.

Another strategy Felix adopts is setting healthy boundaries. He starts politely declining invitations that conflict with his evolving priorities. If a dominant cat insists he join a pointless dispute, Felix refuses, aware that it serves no beneficial purpose. Though it leads to some friction, he finds relief in protecting his time and energy. Boundaries become a form of self-defence against the endless swirl of demands that used to dictate his actions.

A pivotal moment occurs when Felix meets a small group of cats who share a common passion for exploring abandoned structures. Instead of faking interest, he joins them wholeheartedly, finally feeling free to show genuine enthusiasm. Their bond grows from mutual curiosity rather than polite flattery. When disagreements arise, such as who leads the next expedition, they handle it by discussing openly and respecting each other's input, rather than trying to keep everyone complacently happy. This experience shows Felix that healthy relationships can thrive on honesty, disagreement, and collaboration, rather than the brittle veneer of being "nice" at all costs.

Lastly, Felix stops chasing every cat who might offer fleeting praise. He focuses on nurturing bonds with those who appreciate him as he is, while also broadening his capacity to handle polite conflict. You may notice a similar transition in your social life if you stop scattering your energy on winning over everyone and, instead, invest in authentic friendships that grow from shared values or interests. That investment might yield fewer but richer connections.

Over time, these steps change Felix's life. He still values kindness and camaraderie, but he no longer mistakes approval for self-worth. Sometimes he offends a cat who expects blind obedience, but he accepts that. He does not shy away from explaining his viewpoint, nor does he chase after them if they walk away. Each day, he reaffirms that building a life on self-respect feels infinitely more stable than chasing applause that can vanish at any moment.

He also notices that the cats who genuinely respect him offer feedback that helps him grow, rather than shallow compliments. If he attempts a foolish venture, they do not indulge him just to stay on his good side; they voice genuine concern or disagreement. Felix, accustomed to sugary praise, finds this refreshing. Criticism from a trustworthy source spurs improvement, whereas insincere approval merely inflates the ego without substance.

As Felix realises the benefits of living authentically, he senses a new strength developing within him. The tension that once haunted him, whether others might disapprove, eases. He sees that life is precious and too short to squander on endless attempts at popularity. A wave of gratitude washes over him for having learned this truth before the twilight of his fourth life arrives. However, only time will tell if he can fully integrate these changes and avoid yet another last-minute scramble when the end draws near.

Conclusion of Fourth Life

The fourth life of Felix reveals a subtle trap that many overlook. Instead of debilitating fear or tempting comfort, Felix falls into the quest for universal approval. He imagines that being liked will solve his troubles, but the constant craving for acceptance warps his choices and masks his true identity. Only when he glimpses the futility of shaping himself around others' approval does he begin to shift course.

You have watched Felix chase praise, adapting himself to every preference, only to discover that this leads to shallow connections and unrelenting anxiety. The real turning point arrives when he embraces honesty, sets personal milestones, and braves criticism. By climbing that high rooftop for his own reasons, Felix tastes the satisfaction of living by his inner compass. Even the scorn of others no longer shakes him. He learns that genuine friendships arise from shared truths, not unending flattery.

This chapter shows that living for applause can be as damaging as any other stumbling block. Fear immobilises you, comfort dulls you, procrastination steals your time, and approval-seeking robs you of authenticity. Each path ends in regret if you allow it to remain unchecked. Yet Felix has, at last, begun to recognise the worth of being real, even if it means losing the cheap thrill of universal praise. The question remains whether he has learned enough to steer this fourth life to a fulfilling close, or if new challenges will lead him astray again.

In the next chapter, you will see how Felix carries these lessons forward, facing yet another pitfall on the road to a genuinely free and purposeful life. The invitation stands for you to do the same: pause, reflect, and ask yourself whether you, like Felix, have allowed approval-seeking to guide your steps. If so, embrace the power of being true to who you are while your current life still allows it.

The Fifth Life

Aimlessness

You have followed Felix through four distinct lives, each bound by its own stumbling block. He cowered under fear, then dozed in comfort, drifted under procrastination, and finally yearned for approval until he learned to reclaim his authenticity. With every life's end, Felix carried away a handful of lessons. Now, waking in his fifth life, he feels an odd sense of freedom. He is neither paralysed by dread nor desperate for applause, and he knows better than to waste days on trivial delays. The stage seems set for progress.

Yet a new struggle creeps into his mind, one that is not immediately obvious. Felix realises that he lacks direction. Although he has overcome his fixation on others' opinions, he has not replaced it with any genuine goals or inner vision. In trying to avoid his old traps, he drifts from one day to the next, unsure why he should attempt anything beyond gathering food and finding a place to sleep. This subtle aimlessness might be less dramatic than fear or approval-chasing, but it proves every bit as draining.

In this chapter, you will watch as Felix confronts the quiet emptiness of a life lived with no guiding purpose. Through five subheadings, you will see how aimlessness takes root, how it saps motivation, the unseen opportunities it sweeps aside, the philosophical viewpoints that address meaning and direction, and the practical steps to rekindle a sense of purpose. As you turn each page, you might glimpse your own moments of drifting in Felix's story. The question is whether he will recognise that mere survival is not the same as truly living, and whether he can craft a path before another life slips away.

The Quiet Drift into Aimlessness

Imagine Felix slowly rising at dawn in his fifth life. He arches his back, stretches his limbs, and glances around. There is no urgent fear pushing him to hide, nor is he chasing the praise of fellow cats. His memory of previous lives tells him that terror, sloth, approval, and endless postponement lead to regret. So he does neither. Instead, Felix wanders.

At first glance, wandering feels pleasant. He looks at the sky, roams the streets, drinks from puddles, and suns himself on pavement stones. He greets passing cats, but seldom lingers. With no pressing obligations, he can do as he pleases. This freedom appears lovely on a bright morning. Yet as time passes, you notice a pattern: Felix rarely focuses on any task beyond the next meal or the next spot of sunshine. He no longer invests in friendships or challenges, since those require effort and a clear sense of why they matter.

This drift might sound harmless, perhaps even peaceful. You might recall moments in your own life where you felt content to let days flow without strict plans. But as Felix meanders for weeks, a subtle boredom creeps in. He tries half-hearted hunts, occasionally climbs a fence, then shrugs and descends. There is no sense of real achievement, no personal project or bold endeavour to spark his mind. Over time, this emptiness weighs on him, though he struggles to name the cause.

Aimlessness often starts quietly. You shake off big ambitions, telling yourself that chasing goals led to stress in the past.

Aimlessness

You decide to "take life as it comes," believing a relaxed attitude is best. For Felix, his memory of earlier mistakes gives him reason to avoid extremes. He no longer wants to be the cat that leaps into fear, or tries so hard to please others. Yet in avoiding those pitfalls, he adopts a stance of doing very little, drifting through each sunrise and sunset.

You might see parallels in your own routines. Maybe you once aimed for a certain career path or personal dream, only to let it fade. A day here, a week there, and soon months pass without tangible growth or direction. The immediate comfort of drifting holds you, lulling you into repeating the same idle patterns. Like Felix, you might not be unhappy on the surface, yet a quiet dissatisfaction hovers underneath.

What is missing, though not yet obvious to Felix, is a driving sense of purpose. Without purpose, everything feels optional and vaguely unimportant. He hunts when hungry, naps when tired, but invests no energy in bigger pursuits or relationships that might give his life shape. He notices other cats tackling challenges, forming groups, or even training themselves to climb taller structures. Observing them sparks a flicker of curiosity, but then the moment passes, and he meanders off, telling himself that intense involvement can wait.

Social interactions also shift. Because Felix lacks a clear direction, conversations with other cats rarely deepen. He might exchange a polite greeting or share a sunlit patch, but he backs away once deeper topics or plans arise. Fellow cats who have definite aims find him amiable but uninteresting. They might see him as a pleasant drifter, someone who never commits to anything. Over time, these casual connections remain surface-level. The profound bonds that come from shared goals or mutual support never take root.

Oddly, aimlessness can mask itself as freedom. Felix believes he is free from the constraints of fear or people-pleasing. On the surface, he can do what he wants each day. Yet real freedom often involves choosing a path or undertaking meaningful risks. By refusing to define any direction, Felix simply evades responsibility for shaping his life. He does not risk failure, but he also does not attain genuine success. It is a strange limbo: no crisis, no triumph, just a slow parade of identical days.

A more insidious effect is the decline in self-esteem. Every living creature benefits from small victories, catching a challenging prey, forming a supportive bond, or mastering a new skill. Felix, drifting, achieves none of these milestones. While he avoids the sting of defeat or the scorn of others, he also misses the pride that comes from a challenge well met. Gradually, he senses that he is not growing in any direction. This realisation can lead to an undercurrent of depression, though he would not label it as such.

You may notice a subtle exhaustion linked to having no aim. Paradoxically, inactivity can be draining. With no milestones to energise him, Felix's days blur. He sleeps restlessly, uncertain why he should even get up early or stay up late. Nothing tugs at his heart, demanding attention. There is only drifting, moment to moment. At times, you may have experienced a similar apathy, where the absence of goals leaves you oddly tired and unmotivated, even though life is calm.

As you watch Felix in this fifth life, you might recall how each of his previous traps started small and took over. Fear was just a protective instinct until it grew into a prison. Comfort was just a respite until it dulled all ambition. Procrastination was just a minor habit until it devoured his available time. Approval-seeking began as a polite social skill until it became all-consuming. Now, aimlessness starts as a gentle desire to avoid extreme pressures. Before he knows it, it saps his vitality, creating a quiet despair that may claim this life as surely as fear or comfort did in the past.

The key question is whether Felix will detect this drift in time. Will he see that a life without purpose quickly becomes a life without momentum? Or will he continue telling himself that no demands equals bliss, unaware that an unspoken restlessness grows? The following sections explore how aimlessness traps a being in an unfulfilling cycle and whether the lessons from his past might awaken Felix to the necessity of choosing a path, any path before another life dims.

Why We Avoid Purpose

You might ask yourself, "If living with a sense of direction seems so valuable, why would anyone avoid it?" The same puzzle applies to Felix in his aimless state. Deep down, he suspects that pursuing goals might enrich his days, yet he steers clear of any deep commitment. One reason is that purpose carries risk. If you declare a specific aim, you invite the possibility of falling short. Aimlessness lets you sidestep that danger. By never choosing a direction, you never face the sting of failure.

Felix's memories of earlier disappointments feed this mindset. When he sought approval in life four, he discovered how easily praise slipped away. When he set out to conquer tasks in previous lives, he often ended with unfulfilled hopes and regrets. Now, perhaps unconsciously, he thinks that by not committing to a certain goal, he avoids repeating that sadness. He might even tell himself that drifting protects him from future pain.

Another reason we avoid purpose is the fear of making the wrong choice. Felix recalls how picking certain paths earlier led him into traps like procrastination or obsessive approval-seeking. Now, uncertain which direction is best, he chooses none. In your experience, you might have noticed moments of indecision where multiple routes looked equally viable. Rather than risking a poor outcome, you ended up doing nothing. This inactivity can be reassuring in the short term but erodes the chance for meaningful progress.

Additionally, forging a strong purpose demands energy and consistent work. Aimlessness, on the other hand, allows for a lazy kind of existence. Felix might not be proud of it, yet he feels relieved not to push himself. Setting a goal could mean waking earlier, hunting more strategically, learning new skills, or gathering allies. He has no immediate appetite for that exertion. After all, drifting requires no discipline. He convinces himself that calm days suffice, telling himself he is "enjoying life" rather than evading it.

Past traumas also play a role. Felix might still carry unhealed wounds from times he pursued something and ended up feeling foolish or hurt. These memories can breed a protective cynicism: "Why bother aiming high when you can live quietly and avoid heartbreak?" People often echo this sentiment after a failed project or relationship. Instead of addressing the pain, they withdraw from purpose altogether, deciding that half-hearted living is safer than risking heartache again.

Cultural or social factors might reinforce aimlessness as well. If other cats in the vicinity also seem to drift, Felix finds a sort of unspoken peer approval for coasting. There is no shame if everyone else is also unattached to any plan. Belonging to a community that lacks ambition can normalise an idle lifestyle. You might have felt this yourself if you found yourself in a social circle where nobody pursues growth, making you think that drifting is just "the way things are."

Paradoxically, a fear of self-discovery can be another reason. Pursuing a goal or passion can reveal truths about your character and your limits. Aimlessness, by keeping you in a shallow routine, spares you from confronting questions like, "What if I am not as skilled as I hoped?" or "What if my deepest passions require me to leave my comfort zone?" By staying aimless, Felix dodges the vulnerability that comes with self-exploration.

In some cases, we also avoid purpose because of conflicting priorities. You might think, "I have too many potential directions, so I will pick none." Felix might see multiple interesting paths, maybe forming a new hunting collective, exploring further territories, or supporting weaker cats, but he cannot decide which is best. Instead of choosing one, he chooses none, drifting without a firm anchor. Each passing day, the wealth of possibilities ironically ensures none are pursued.

Aimlessness can thus become a self-reinforcing cycle. The longer you drift, the less confidence you have in your ability to commit. Observing how others achieve milestones might spark envy, but it also heightens the sense that you have fallen behind. Felix might think, "They are already so far ahead, I cannot catch up now." This thought further cements his reluctance to start anything. In the end, aimlessness feels like the lesser evil, avoiding both competition and potential embarrassment.

Felix, if questioned, might pretend he is content. After all, he experiences no major drama or stress. Yet behind that façade lies a faint awareness that each day ends without meaningful progress. Sometimes, aimlessness grows from the residue of earlier chapters. Felix might recall how he used to chase illusions like universal approval. Disillusioned by that experience, he has decided that chasing anything else could be just another trap. So he remains stuck, not realising that genuine purpose differs from hollow distractions.

Ultimately, these reasons highlight that avoiding purpose is seldom just laziness; it can be rooted in self-protection, fear of commitment, or unresolved hurt. For Felix, all these elements swirl in his subconscious, steering him away from deeper ambitions. In the next section, you will see how the consequences of such a life manifest, revealing that even though aimlessness seems harmless, it can quietly strip a life of its colour and leave one grappling with a sense of emptiness that is hard to shake off.

The Consequences of Living Without Direction

Although Felix feels no acute crisis, the subtle results of aimlessness begin to press on him. Days blur into one another with little to mark their passing. Even his recollection of where he ventured or which cats he met becomes hazy since nothing stands out. Over time, this robs him of that vibrancy which once surfaced whenever he tackled a fresh idea or overcame an obstacle.

One of the first clear effects is the erosion of self-worth. You may recall that self-esteem often grows when you master

Aimlessness

skills, achieve small goals, or contribute to the community. Because Felix avoids challenges, he never tests or expands his capabilities. Eventually, he doubts his own potential, telling himself he probably would not excel at anything anyway. This self-doubt then justifies further inaction, forming a loop that keeps him drifting.

Another consequence is missed opportunities. Life does not stand still, even if Felix does. Others discover new feeding grounds or form alliances that lead them to safer, richer habitats. Meanwhile, Felix hears about these developments only in passing, too late to join or too uninvolved to make the effort. Where he once might have carved out a niche or built lasting bonds, he remains a bystander. Opportunities that could have enriched his existence slip away unclaimed.

Aimlessness also breeds a shallow social existence. Felix, with no particular direction, struggles to connect deeply with those who have clear ambitions. Such cats often move forward, forging close ties with partners who share their goals. Felix, unwilling to invest in any plan or cause, lingers on the sidelines. He has acquaintances but not many real companions. Over time, this partial isolation saps his spirits. A sense of emptiness creeps in as he realises how rarely he partakes in shared experiences that foster genuine closeness.

A more insidious outcome is the slow onset of listlessness. While Felix is free from immediate stress, he also feels little motivation to rise each morning. Sometimes, he sleeps longer than necessary, as there is nothing compelling awaiting him. You might recognise that feeling of staying in bed because no plan or duty tugs at you. This state can lead to mild despair, a background sorrow that something vital is missing. Felix avoids calling it depression, but the signs are there: low energy, low interest, and a muted curiosity.

You see, a purposeful life is not merely about grand achievements. Even small daily objectives infuse your routine with meaning. If you aim to learn a new technique or help a neighbour, you approach the day with a bit more purpose. Felix, lacking such aims, wanders like a leaf on the wind. By sundown, he cannot point to anything he truly learned or contributed. The day ends as it started, and the cycle repeats.

This drifting also makes Felix vulnerable to unexpected upheaval. With no network or plan to fall back on a sudden challenge can leave him unprepared. If hostile cats move into his area or a food source runs dry, Felix might scramble, realising too late that he has neglected forming alliances or scouting new territories. Without direction, he never invests in resilience, so when change comes, and it always does, he finds himself starting from scratch.

Emotionally, a void settles in. Felix occasionally glimpses other cats returning from shared ventures, eyes bright with stories of risk and discovery. He feels a pang of envy. Although he avoided the friction that can come with strong goals, he also missed out on the rewards. That glimpse of what he could have had intensifies his lurking sadness. He sees that simply avoiding pitfalls does not guarantee fulfilment. A life with no major mistakes can still end up hollow.

Like many negative patterns, aimlessness can also mask deeper issues. Perhaps Felix is worried that any chosen path might echo his old failures. Or he might be too jaded to believe in a meaningful quest. Because he never confronts these internal blockages, they remain unresolved, intensifying his reluctance to try anything new. Meanwhile, time passes.

If you have felt this type of ennui, you know how easy it is to continue drifting. There is no single crisis forcing you to act, so each day, you say, "I'll figure out a direction tomorrow." This approach ironically resembles Felix's old procrastination cycle, except that he is not even naming a task to delay. He simply wanders, telling himself life is fine. Yet deep inside, a whisper reminds him that life is more than mere survival. That whisper grows louder with each passing week, telling him to shape his path before the clock runs out.

In a cat's perspective, nine lives might sound abundant, but Felix has already used four. Even if he does not dwell on mortality, somewhere within him lurks the memory that his days can end unexpectedly. This knowledge should, ideally, prompt him to live more deliberately. Yet aimlessness has dulled that sense of urgency. Without conscious effort, Felix floats through each dawn, ignoring the silent reality that the days of this fifth life are finite.

Thus, the consequences of living without direction are both subtle and potent. Over many seasons, aimlessness can degrade confidence, diminish relationships, and strip life of significance. If Felix continues on this path, he risks arriving at the twilight of his fifth life, shocked by how little he has to show for it. The next section will explore the philosophical insights that might awaken him to the necessity of forging a meaning, even if it is imperfect before another precious life is spent.

Philosophical Insights on Purpose

Throughout his earlier lives, Felix encountered philosophical teachings on fear, comfort, procrastination, and approval. Now, as he drifts in aimlessness, these viewpoints can guide him again if only he recalls them. Many thinkers across cultures have grappled with the question of purpose, offering insights that resonate with cats and humans alike.

Existential perspectives propose that meaning is not automatically handed to you; you must create it. In Felix's case, waiting for some external sign or push to define his life is futile. He must choose a direction, even if it feels artificial at first. By acting on that chosen path, the meaning emerges. Existential philosophers argue that although life has no built-in script, you can generate purpose through decisions, however small. Felix, if he truly grasped this, would see that drifting is a choice as much as purposeful movement is.

Stoic traditions remind us that we control only our actions and reactions, not external forces. Aimlessness often stems from the belief that if there is no grand destiny, there is no point in effort. Yet the Stoics would say your duty is to harness your inner power, living in accordance with virtue or reason, regardless of life's external shape. Felix could adopt a routine of daily improvement, be it honing a hunting skill or supporting weaker cats, finding purpose in the discipline of self-directed growth. Whether external events favour him or not, he can derive meaning from consistent effort.

From an Eastern outlook, purpose can be seen as alignment with the natural flow, yet that does not equate to passive drifting. In Taoist thought, there is a notion of effortless action, but it arises when you act in harmony with life's rhythms. Felix might misinterpret drifting as "going with the flow," but real harmony involves awareness, responsiveness, and a certain intention. Passive wandering usually neglects the deeper engagement that Taoist teachings emphasise.

Meanwhile, other philosophies highlight contribution as a path to meaning. Some forms of humanistic thinking argue that you find purpose when you serve something beyond yourself, a cause, a community, or a creative pursuit. Felix might discover direction by mentoring younger cats, collaborating on a shared goal, or improving conditions for felines in a tough area. Rather than drifting, he would channel his energy into a mission that transcends his individual appetites.

A recurring motif across these schools is that purpose is seldom grand or perfect from the start. You do not need to wait for a life-altering vision. Instead, you begin with small commitments, test them, and refine your path. By avoiding any start, you forfeit the chance to learn which pursuits resonate with you. Felix, floating around, might try volunteering to guard a communal food source or exploring a seldom-visited park. Even if these attempts feel modest, they can spark momentum and reveal new passions.

Another point is that self-reflection matters. Philosophical thinkers, from Socrates to Buddhist teachers, champion introspection as the root of meaningful living. Felix might benefit from quiet moments, not to doze but to ask, "What do I value? What do I find worthwhile?" Even if his answers are uncertain, the act of questioning nudges him out of apathy. You might do the same in your life, journaling or sitting quietly to discern what genuinely animates you beyond your basic needs.

Purpose is also linked to mortality awareness. Felix, on some level, knows his lives are not infinite. Many philosophers emphasise that realising life's brevity can motivate you to use your days wisely. If Felix faced this fact squarely, he might hurry to invest in something meaningful rather than squander hours on aimless wandering. A healthy grasp of impermanence can cut through complacency, urging us to act while we still can.

The final highlight from these teachings is that purpose need not be solitary. Collaborative projects, shared adventures, or communal endeavours often yield deeper fulfilment than purely individual aims. For Felix, forging strong alliances around a mutual goal could combine the social aspect he sometimes neglects with a renewed sense of direction. If a group wants to safeguard an area from rival cats or gather resources for kittens, Felix might channel his energy into that, gaining camaraderie and purpose in one stroke.

In summary, philosophical insights suggest that waiting for a perfect or preordained calling only prolongs drift. Felix, if he embraces these ideas, must take a small leap of faith: choose a modest aim, act upon it, and stay open to refining it. Through trial, reflection, and acceptance of imperfection, he can generate the sense of meaning that his aimless days lack. Whether that purpose is spiritual, communal, or self-improvement, it offers a reason to rise each dawn with a quiet determination rather than a resigned shrug.

If Felix recalls this wisdom, he can break free from the grey routine overshadowing his fifth life. The next section will show how he might rekindle focus and meaning through practical steps, turning aimlessness into motivation for a brighter chapter if he acts in time.

Aimlessness

Rekindling Focus and Meaning

Once Felix senses the hollowness of aimlessness, he stands at a crossroads: accept a quiet drift toward yet another wasted life or seek a path that sparks his heart. Although it feels daunting, the memory of past regrets urges him to at least try. He recalls how, in each preceding life, a change of mindset came too late. This time, he hopes to seize the chance before the final hours loom.

His first move is to define a simple, doable target. Rather than fantasising about a grand transformation, Felix picks something tangible: he decides to improve his hunting skills so he can assist weaker cats who struggle for food. While he is far from heroic in this goal, it gives structure to his mornings: he wakes with a reason to train. At dawn, he practises pouncing or sprinting after small creatures, sharpening reflexes that have dulled from drifting. Already, the day gains more colour. He has a purpose, even if it is just honing a skill, and that aim encourages him to push himself a bit further each session.

Second, Felix arranges to meet a cat named Rowan, an old acquaintance who values cooperation. They plan brief scouting trips to corners of the neighbourhood, Felix has ignored in his aimless wanders. Together, they note new shelters or potential threats, building a sense of shared endeavour. While these expeditions are modest, they infuse Felix's routine with camaraderie and anticipation. Each meeting spurs him to keep going, knowing Rowan relies on him to show up. This accountability helps resist the pull of idle drifting.

Another step is self-reflection. At night, Felix sits by a quiet fence and asks, "How did I spend my time today? Did I advance my hunting practice? Did I honour my goal to assist others?" He does not ruminate harshly but uses this as a friendly check-in. On days he slacks off, the simple act of noticing it prevents mindless repetition. You might adopt a similar habit, writing down your daily activities to track whether you moved toward or away from a chosen aim. It is not about obsessing over achievements but staying mindful enough to avoid slipping back into apathy.

Felix also experiments with larger projects. When he hears of kittens rummaging for scraps near a dangerous road, he sees a chance to contribute. Gathering a few allies, he helps guide the kittens to a safer spot and shows them where to find a more consistent food source. This involvement proves more challenging than his personal hunting drills, but it sparks a sense of satisfaction he has not felt in a long while. He realises that assisting others or solving small crises can fill each day with a unique sense of purpose, far richer than wandering aimlessly.

Inevitably, Felix faces setbacks. He might fail to catch anything worthwhile for days, questioning whether his chosen focus is misguided. He might grow lazy on a cold morning, skipping practice to doze in an abandoned garden. Yet, each time, he recalls the emptiness that haunted him. This memory pushes him to renew his vow, even if it means taking smaller steps when he feels demotivated. Instead of slipping back into aimlessness at the first hurdle, he learns the value of resilience. Purpose, he discovers, is not about never faltering but about returning to the path after a stumble.

A critical element is letting go of the expectation that every day must be monumental. Felix understands that some days produce only minor progress or fleeting achievements. Yet even such modest gains accumulate. By week's end, he sees that he has practised hunting more hours than the previous one, or guided another lost kitten to shelter. These small wins fuel self-belief. Over time, he feels his sense of identity shifting: from a drifter to a cat with a role, however humble, in the neighbourhood's wellbeing.

Felix also notices the benefits for his relationships. Other cats, seeing his consistent dedication, start to respect him more. They offer to help or share knowledge, sensing that he is serious about contributing. A few even commend his efforts openly, though Felix now knows better than to depend on their praise. The difference is that he does not chase their admiration; he focuses on the task itself. This shift from external validation to internal purpose fosters deeper ties built on mutual interests rather than shallow flattery.

In parallel, Felix's own mind clears. He wakes with a plan and rests at night with some sense of accomplishment, large or small. The haze of drifting recedes. He may not always relish the routine; some days, he yearns to lounge idly, but the overall structure gives him a balance of rest and productivity. The repeated practice of making choices aligned with a purpose shapes his life, forging a narrative that is no longer blank.

Another insight he gains is that purpose can evolve. Maybe, in time, he will outgrow the current goals and shift to something else. That does not invalidate his present focus. Instead, it reminds him that meaning is fluid. The key is to remain engaged and to choose directions as life changes rather than reverting to aimless wandering. He realises that the worst mistake is not picking an "imperfect" aim but refusing to pick any aim at all.

Finally, Felix reaffirms that failures along the way do not mean he should abandon direction. When a hunting attempt goes poorly, or a rescue mission fails to help every kitten, he resists the old urge to shrug and quit. Instead, he learns from mistakes, adjusting his technique or seeking guidance from more experienced cats. Each challenge, even the painful ones, feeds into a larger sense of ongoing purpose. He realises that a life dedicated to meaningful actions, even if flawed, is more vibrant than an existence of aimless tranquillity.

As he integrates these steps, Felix feels a renewed spark of life. Although he is far from perfect, he no longer greets each morning with blank indifference. He has found a direction worth walking, and that alone rescues him from the slow suffocation of drifting. Yet the clock continues to tick in this fifth life, leaving you to wonder if Felix will hold onto this course until the end or if fresh obstacles will threaten to unravel his newfound meaning.

Conclusion of Fifth Life

Felix's fifth life reveals a quiet danger that can be just as corrosive as any fierce battle, living without aim. Drifting day by day might feel harmless, but it gradually drains your energy and potential. You have witnessed how Felix, free from old pitfalls, still risks squandering his life by avoiding direction. Through introspection, small goals, and collaborative efforts, he discovers that a modest sense of purpose transforms ordinary days into a journey worth taking.

Aimlessness

The key insight is that aimlessness often appears soft and benign, yet it slowly erodes self-esteem, opportunities, and meaningful relationships. When Felix finally recognises the hollow nature of his aimless wandering, he grasps that defining even a humble purpose can rekindle enthusiasm and fulfilment. Each dawn brings a chance to practise his skills or assist another cat, and each evening closes with the glow of minor achievements.

Whether you identify with Felix's drift or not, his story underlines that mere survival is not enough. Purpose does not need to be grand or flawless, but it must exist if you are to escape the subtle emptiness of directionless living. Felix's late awakening in this fifth life shows that picking a path, any path can restore the vibrant drive that once flickered out under the cloak of complacency. If he holds to this lesson, he may end his fifth life without the weighty regrets that have stained earlier chapters. Yet only time will reveal how deeply these lessons take root and whether, when faced with fresh challenges, Felix's newfound focus can carry him toward a brighter close to his story.

The Sixth Life

Regret

You have journeyed with Felix through five lives, each bound by its own barrier. He trembled under fear, lounged in comfort, fell behind through procrastination, chased approval, and drifted in aimlessness. Yet each time, he managed a moment of clarity that hinted he might turn things around. Now, beginning his sixth existence, Felix finds an unexpected spectre clinging to his tail: regret.

Regret stalks Felix quietly at first, showing up as fleeting thoughts when he recalls the many lost moments in past lives. He thinks of bold actions never taken, friendships left incomplete, and days wasted on trivial distractions. Though Felix tries to focus on the present, these memories resurface, stealing the taste from his meals and the joy from his wanderings. The gnawing sense that he has squandered chances drags behind him like a heavy chain. You might understand the feeling, those moments when old mistakes or ignored opportunities make you flinch inside.

This chapter follows Felix as regret overshadows his actions, influencing how he moves through the streets and interacts with fellow cats. Through five subheadings, you will see how regret becomes both a burden and a potential teacher: where it arises, why it can paralyse you, how it dims motivation, the philosophical angles that illuminate it, and the methods Felix might use to transform regret into a driving force rather than a cage. With each section, you may recognise echoes of your own regrets, or find insight into how to address them. The question remains whether Felix can see regret as a prompt for change, or if it will become an excuse to sink into despair. In a life already shaped by unfulfilled chances, will regret deliver the final blow, or point him toward a better path?

The Shadow of Missed Opportunities

Felix begins his sixth life feeling oddly burdened, even though nothing particularly ominous troubles him in the present. He roams as any cat would, seeking food and safety, but there is a slight hesitation in his steps. New sights remind him of old paths not taken, while friendly meows from passing felines stir memories of conversations he never finished. It is as if his past choices float around him in the air. In quiet moments, a wave of melancholy envelops him.

These missed opportunities are varied. He thinks of the orchard he never fully explored, the alliance with Rowan that he failed to strengthen, and the kittens he once intended to guide yet never revisited. Each recollection pinches his heart. He recalls how, at the time, he told himself he would act later or that circumstances were not quite right. Now, he sees how those excuses robbed him of experiences that might have enriched his earlier lives. As the days unfold, these regrets stack up, forming a constant backdrop to his waking hours.

You might have felt something similar: a chance to learn a skill or deepen a relationship left on the back burner, until it withered unfulfilled. The memory still stings. That ache is regret. In Felix's case, the sting resonates through multiple lives, intensifying his sense of waste. Each time he glimpses a new corner of the neighbourhood, he wonders if it is another orchard he will never revisit, another chance that might slip away. Consequently, Felix grows more cautious. Instead of boldness, he allows regret to dampen his enthusiasm. He feels he has failed too often in the past to approach new ventures with the excitement he once had.

Regret does not simply highlight a past omission; it also saps present motivation. Felix sometimes sees a group of cats training for a tricky climb, and a spark of curiosity lights within him. Almost at once, he recalls the climbs he avoided before, followed by the remorse he now harbours. "Why bother trying?" he thinks. "I might only repeat the pattern and regret it even more later." This self-defeating mindset underscores how regret can create fresh missed opportunities. It becomes a loop: you feel sorrow for old choices, which leads you to stall on new ones, which eventually spawn further regrets.

Another side effect is the skewing of memory. Felix fixates on his failures, minimising the instances where he did act. He recalls all the fences he never scaled; while forgetting the few times he showed courage. Regret acts like a magnifying mirror, enlarging every shortfall. This distorted view intensifies his guilt, making him underestimate his capacity for change. It is as if regret emphasises the negative, overshadowing the reality that he has, on occasion, succeeded or at least improved.

Socially, regret can breed distance. Felix grows reluctant to share his recollections or confide in friends, worried they will judge him for past mistakes. He might sidestep gatherings or keep conversation superficial, unwilling to reveal the heavy sense of guilt lurking within. Over time, this limits emotional support that could have helped him break free from regret's grip. You might have experienced this as well: letting shame about old blunders keep you from genuine connection, unaware that vulnerability might bring solace or new insight.

Regret

In your own life, regrets can range from small missteps to significant turning points, each one chipping away at your self-assurance if left unaddressed. For Felix, they accumulate like stones in a sack he carries from dawn to dusk. Sometimes these regrets galvanise him to reflect, but more often they freeze him in place, as he imagines how he could fail or overlook something yet again. This prevents any forward momentum, making each day a continuation of sorrow for all that is gone.

Gradually, Felix's demeanour changes. He speaks less, moves more slowly, and shies away from suggestions or offers of help. It is not that fear has returned exactly, but regret exerts a similar grip, whispering that he has already squandered too many lives, so why push himself to do better now? In this sense, regret forms a dark shadow that blocks out hope. Rather than using it as a sign to act differently, Felix wears it like a burden that weighs him down, stalling any attempt at progress.

Yet regret also holds a seed of wisdom. The very fact that Felix mourns missed opportunities suggests he values growth or connection, even if he once neglected them. If he harnessed that realisation, regret could evolve from an anchor into a catalyst. He could examine why he avoided certain risks, vow to approach them differently, and use the memory of guilt as fuel to drive future action. The potential for transformation lies beneath the discomfort, but only if he finds the courage to face these past lapses without sinking into despair.

This tension is at the heart of regret: it can close you off or it can open you up. Felix currently experiences the closing effect. Each missed chance morphs into a reason not to try. However, he stands on a threshold. Should he decide to examine his regrets, glean their lessons, and begin anew, he might still steer this sixth life in a promising direction. If he delays much longer, the shadow of missed opportunities may just devour another life entirely, leaving him deeper in sorrow than ever before.

As you follow his story, you may identify times when your own regrets felt too big to confront. Perhaps you too stalled, replaying old scenarios. Yet regret remains a universal phenomenon, and many who have faced it uncover a chance for redemption by turning that sorrow into motivation. Whether Felix finds that chance, or remains chained to his remorse, will shape the remainder of this sixth life. For now, the missed opportunities swirl around him, demanding a reckoning he is not sure he can handle.

The Anatomy of Regret

You might question what makes regret such a potent force in Felix's sixth life. After all, his earlier journeys show that emotions like fear or complacency can derail him, but regret carries its own unique weight. To understand why, you need to look at regret's psychological roots, the way it weaves past actions (or inactions) into a narrative of sorrow, and how it warps present perception.

On the most basic level, regret arises when you believe you could have made a different choice that would have led to a better outcome. Felix sees a new orchard or a group of exploring cats, recalls how he once failed to engage fully, and imagines how different things might have been if he had acted. This imagined better path intensifies his dissatisfaction with the real path he chose. The more vivid the contrast, the sharper the regret.

Regret

Regret is also tied to a sense of personal responsibility. Felix cannot blame external factors alone for his unfulfilled ambitions; deep down, he knows his own hesitation or inattention led to certain missed chances. A dog's bark or another cat's hostility might have been obstacles, but ultimately, he realises he had a hand in turning away. This self-blame deepens the sting, leaving him feeling complicit in his own misery.

In many cases, regret grows larger over time. Immediately after skipping an opportunity, you might shrug and think, "Next time." But as years or lives pass, the accumulation of these casual dismissals weighs more heavily. Felix now stands in his sixth life, reflecting on an entire mosaic of undone activities. Each small regret merges into a formidable arrangement, overshadowing the modest successes he did achieve.

Each small regret merges into a grand arrangement of regretful memories, overshadowing the modest successes he did achieve.

Another critical element of regret is the emotional swirl it creates. Felix might experience guilt for wasting potential, sadness for what he missed, and frustration that he cannot travel back to fix anything. Sometimes regret even mingles with anger, especially if he blames older versions of himself for being lazy or fearful. This cocktail of guilt, grief, and ire can sap emotional energy, leaving little left for present endeavours.

Regret also feeds on comparison. Felix sees younger cats bravely venturing out, forming new alliances, and building stories he will never match. In your own life, you might feel regret most strongly when you see how a friend or colleague advanced in a direction you once yearned to pursue but did not. This comparison emphasises the gap between what is and what might have been, intensifying the ache. Felix, noticing how others progressed where he stalled, feels even more deflated.

Then there is the matter of identity. Regret influences self-perception. When you frequently ruminate on past failings, you start to label yourself as someone who "always messes up" or "never follows through." This negative identity can become a self-fulfilling prophecy, dissuading you from trying new paths because you assume you will only fail again. Felix slips into this mindset, concluding that his regrets prove he is a cat who cannot seize chances, so why bother now?

Interestingly, regret can also be rooted in longing for lost relationships. Felix occasionally thinks of the cats he drifted away from or the ones he disappointed by not keeping promises. He wonders what alliances could have formed if he had stayed consistent. That relational aspect of regret stings because it reminds him that missed opportunities can also mean missed companionship, which is harder to quantify than a missed meal or a lost vantage point.

Philosophers often point out that regret is retrospective, fixating on a past that cannot be changed. For Felix, repeatedly playing old scenes in his mind does nothing to alter those events. The real question is how he will live now, yet the emotional magnetism of regret draws his thoughts backward. You might recognise this loop in your own internal monologue, replaying a mistake instead of focusing on the present or future. This backward pull can become so strong that you feel immobilised.

Regret

Some blame external circumstances to minimise regret: "I had no choice," or "The timing was bad." But Felix cannot lie to himself that thoroughly. He sees that many small decisions stacked up to shape his path. A sense of personal agency, ironically, intensifies regret by reinforcing that he could have done otherwise but did not. If there were no sense of choice, regret would not bite so hard. The presence of choice and the awareness of it being squandered give regret its razor-sharp edge.

In short, regret emerges from the belief that different actions could have altered outcomes for the better, coupled with a feeling of personal accountability and a longing for what was never experienced. This combination is potent, overshadowing daily life with "what if" scenarios. For Felix, each new dawn carries the echo of old mornings when he never mustered the courage or drive to do more. If left unresolved, regret can become an ever-present murmur that shapes how he sees himself, others, and the world.

Yet, paradoxically, the depth of regret also testifies to the fact that Felix does care about living fully. If he did not, he would not feel this longing for what might have been. Recognising that regret grows from valuing certain experiences can transform it into motivation. If he acts upon what he missed, forging new commitments or amends, he may discover that regret is not a terminal sentence but a prompt to realign his path. That remains to be seen; for now, regret is winning the internal tug-of-war, leaving Felix weighed down by the life that could have been.

How Regret Stifles Growth

Felix's regret is not just a painful recollection; it also shapes his outlook on the future. Like a cat skulking in the shadows, it lurks in each corner of his mind. As a result, he hesitates to invest in new projects or friendships, convinced that any attempt will end up as one more line in his litany of mistakes. In effect, regret stifles growth by replacing curiosity with caution and hope with cynicism.

One immediate impact is a crisis of self-belief. Felix thinks, "If I messed up so many times before, why would now be different?" This question alone can stop him from even trying. Each missed chance in the past becomes evidence for a future failure. Regret morphs from an emotion tied to specific memories into a general statement about his capabilities. In your own experience, you might have seen how fixating on prior mistakes can blind you to progress you have made or can still make.

Another way regret stifles growth is by narrowing Felix's vision. Instead of scanning horizons for opportunities, he remains fixated on the rear-view mirror. He might spot a new orchard or a fledgling group of cats planning something exciting, but regret's whisper reminds him of the orchard he never finished exploring or the alliances he neglected. This relentless backward gaze robs him of the imaginative spark needed to engage with fresh possibilities.

Socially, regret can sabotage constructive bonds. Felix might be reluctant to show vulnerability, believing others will judge him for his past lapses. He keeps interactions light, rarely opening up about deeper hopes or fears. While this strategy protects him from immediate embarrassment, it also prevents any genuine support or encouragement that might help him move beyond his regrets. He never discovers that many cats carry their own burdens and could empathise if given the chance.

You might notice that regret often creates a double-bind: the more you regret your inaction, the less likely you are to break the pattern and act now. The emotional weight fosters a sense of inevitability, as if you are doomed to keep repeating the same errors. This fatalism undercuts any motivation to attempt something bold. It is simpler, though emptier, to remain in a safe corner, licking old wounds and sighing over what might have been.

Physically, regret can lead to lethargy. Felix may not starve, but he invests minimal energy in tasks that once intrigued him. His hunts become half-hearted, lacking the zeal he displayed in earlier lives when curiosity or ambition drove him to excel. This slowdown feeds a loop: with no purposeful drive, each day's outcomes fail to spark pride, which in turn deepens the sense that he is wasting another life. He experiences a gradual decline in stamina and zest, attributing it to age or external factors, when in truth regret saps his will.

Moreover, regret reduces resilience. When a setback arises, Felix recalls all his prior missteps and sees them as confirmation that he cannot recover. A cat more free from regret might respond, "This is tough, but I can adapt." Felix, tangled in remorse, tells himself it is just another sign that he is incapable of improvement. This negative self-talk drains the determination needed to bounce back. Over time, even small challenges feel insurmountable.

From a broader perspective, regret narrows what psychologists call your "possibility frame." If you define yourself as someone who always fails to seize the moment, you fail to notice smaller steps that could inch you forward.

You might interpret open doors as closed, or misread tentative invitations as certain rejections. Felix often wanders by a group of cats planning an adventure, but he imagines they would mock or ignore him because he is "the one who never follows through." He does not ask, so he never learns that they might welcome him.

At its worst, regret can sour your attitude toward life entirely. Felix occasionally lapses into a sullen mood, feeling each sunrise as a burden rather than a gift. The cynicism that grows from regret paints everything dull. You might liken this to a cat that once viewed the neighbourhood with curiosity, now seeing only monotony and ghosts of what could have been. In this mindset, new ventures appear pointless and even the simplest pleasures ring hollow.

Yet regret does not have to remain a dead weight. It only stifles growth when it overwhelms any faith in present or future potential. If Felix found a way to reframe regret as a call to action, it might propel him to seize the day instead of mourning yesterday. He could recall each missed orchard or undone climb and think, "I feel remorse precisely because I value those experiences, so let me act now before it is truly too late." That would turn regret into a teacher.

For the moment, Felix has not chosen that path. He trudges along, convinced that his best opportunities lie behind him, overshadowed by the gloom of repeated regrets. You can see how this conviction robs him of the very growth that might banish regret. The chapters ahead in this life hinge on whether he can break that vicious circle. If regret is left to fester, he may waste the sixth life lamenting the first five. If he harnesses its lessons, he might yet salvage a portion of these days, forging a future no longer bound by sorrow for the past.

Regret

Philosophical Reflections on Regret

Like all of Felix's struggles, regret can be viewed through the lens of great philosophical traditions. Many thinkers have wrestled with how to handle remorse for what has passed. Their conclusions often revolve around acceptance, learning, and a recognition that life continues forward, not backward.

Stoic philosophy, for example, highlights the importance of focusing on what lies within your control. Past actions, having already occurred, rest outside that boundary. A Stoic might counsel Felix to note his old missteps, accept they cannot be undone, and then direct attention to what can be influenced now. This mindset does not trivialise regret, but it reframes it as historical fact rather than an ongoing chain around his neck.

From an existential angle, regret underscores personal responsibility. Felix regrets his inaction precisely because he knows he had choices. Existentialists suggest that rather than denying this responsibility, you can embrace it. If your freedom led you to neglect opportunities, that same freedom can be used today to make better choices. While the weight of regret might feel crushing, it also proves you are not just a passive bystander in your life. You have the power to alter your path.

Buddhist-influenced teachings emphasise the notion of impermanence. Everything, including your regrets, constantly shifts. If Felix recognises that each moment is new, he might see regret as an attachment to a story that no longer exists. The past has dissolved, so clinging to it yields suffering. Letting go does not mean ignoring lessons, but rather releasing the emotional torment that keeps him trapped. This perspective encourages compassion for oneself: you acted with limited insight at the time. Now, you can act with greater understanding.

Another relevant viewpoint is that regret can highlight deeper values. You only regret ignoring something if it truly mattered to you. For Felix, the orchard or alliances he never pursued were genuinely significant. By recognising that regret surfaces where your real interests lie, you gain a chance to refocus. If Felix's heart aches for missed exploration, it reveals how crucial exploration is to him. Perhaps he can use that revelation to shape his current actions.

Philosophical thought also questions the utility of regret. If it provokes you to do better, it can be a useful motivator. However, if it paralyses you, it becomes mere rumination that hinders growth. Ancient and modern thinkers alike suggest balancing reflection with forward-looking energy. A measured dose of regret prompts accountability, while an overdose smothers hope. Felix, if he studied these ideas, might see that regret is neither inherently good nor evil, but a tool that can guide or hamper him depending on his approach.

Acceptance is another key theme. Some schools stress that regrets often arise from ignoring life's unpredictability. We imagine we had total control of outcomes, though chance and timing often play roles. Felix might have overlooked that circumstances in previous lives did not entirely lie under his command. Accepting that partial unpredictability can lighten the self-blame and free him to commit wholeheartedly to what remains possible now, rather than drowning in what might have been.

A final philosophical insight is that regret can be integrated into a broader personal narrative. Instead of seeing it as a list of errors, you fold it into your ongoing story. You accept that you are not the same cat you were. Your regrets become chapters that shaped your perspective, fuelling empathy or a clearer sense of priorities. If Felix merges his regrets into a renewed mission—helping younger cats avoid the same pitfalls or fully exploring hidden gardens now—he transforms regret into a stepping stone.

These reflections echo across cultures and eras, reminding you that regret is a shared human (or feline) experience. It signals that you cared about something enough to wish you had done more. Rather than letting it remain pure sorrow, you can channel it. Felix's challenge lies in seeing this potential. If he remains mired in self-reproach, the pages of his sixth life may fill with bitterness. If he applies these philosophical insights, he might accept the unchangeable past, glean its lessons, and act decisively.

The gap between regret as a shackle and regret as a catalyst is not large, but crossing it requires intention. Felix will need to push himself to revisit old wounds, glean the moral of each story, and decide that those regrets will no longer rule him. That might mean apologising to cats he let down, pursuing activities he once neglected, or forging brand-new objectives. Each act of purposeful living helps regret shift from a destructive force to a reminder of what truly matters, revealing a path forward that resonates with genuine purpose.

Transforming Regret into Resolve

Felix reaches a crossroads when regret grows too heavy to ignore. Either he sinks under its weight, letting it define him, or he finds a method to transform his remorse into a dynamic force that drives him onward. The first step is an honest audit of his regrets. Instead of letting them swirl in vague sorrow, he lists them mentally: the orchard he never finished exploring, the training sessions he abandoned, the alliances he neglected, and so on. By naming them, he shines a light on each, no longer letting them fester in the dark.

This inventory stings, yet it also brings clarity. He sees patterns in his behaviour: perhaps he used to give up too soon or avoided discomfort whenever it arose. You might do a similar exercise, writing down your regrets to see if a common thread unites them. Through this process, Felix realises that his regrets often revolve around backing away the moment challenges became real. Identifying this pattern paves the way for mindful change.

Second, Felix picks one regret to address in a concrete way. For instance, he recalls an old friend, Rowan, whom he once promised to join on an expedition but never did. Rather than wallowing in shame, he resolves to find Rowan and apologise, then propose a new plan. This single action, even if humble, moves regret from idle lament to purposeful restitution. If Rowan is willing to give him another chance, Felix can make amends by showing genuine commitment this time.

You might see how focusing on one regret at a time prevents overwhelm. Rather than trying to fix everything at once, you choose a manageable point of entry that can begin to shift your overall mindset. It also combats the all-or-nothing approach that regret often fosters. Each redeemed opportunity lessens the sense of helplessness, planting seeds of confidence that you are not doomed to keep failing.

Third, Felix sets fresh, forward-looking goals that honour his unfulfilled yearnings. If he regrets never exploring certain rooftops, he decides to do so now, naming specific spots to visit each week. If he regrets ignoring younger cats, he volunteers to teach them the hunting techniques he has learned. This approach acknowledges that the past cannot be changed, but the values underlying those regrets can still be honoured. You might adopt the same stance, realising that while you cannot undo old mistakes, you can still act today in a way that reflects what truly matters to you.

An important component is self-forgiveness. Felix recognises that he once acted with limited awareness, fear, or distraction. Those choices shaped his regrets, but if he clings to self-condemnation, he will never move on. Through quiet introspection, he releases the harsh blame that kept him chained to the past. This does not absolve him of accountability for what he missed, but it frees him from the toxic cycle of punishing himself endlessly. He learns to see regret as a teacher rather than a prison guard.

Alongside self-forgiveness, Felix shares parts of his story with those he trusts. Maybe he confides in a fellow cat about how deeply his missed orchard journey gnaws at him. By opening up, he discovers empathy or advice he never anticipated. This shared reflection can further dissolve regret's isolating hold. You might mirror this, confiding in a friend or mentor about regrets that loom large and finding that honest dialogue can lighten the load.

Felix also makes peace with imperfection. He realises not every regret can be fully repaired. Perhaps certain cats have moved on, or certain chances are gone for good. In these cases, he focuses on what he can do now. If the orchard is destroyed or changed, he looks for another location that satisfies his thirst for exploration. The acceptance that some regrets cannot be undone helps him direct energy into new territory rather than fruitless longing for a perfect redo.

Finally, Felix incorporates a daily ritual of reflection to keep regrets from stealthily returning. Each evening, he briefly reviews the day, praising small steps forward and noticing any fresh lapses that could become new regrets if unaddressed. By staying alert, he stops the cycle of ignoring opportunities. A day where he overcame reluctance or finished a task, no matter how small, becomes a day free of regret. You can adopt a similar practice, ensuring regrets do not accumulate unheeded.

Through these actions, regret gradually morphs from a paralysing force into a motivator for improvement. Felix, once weighed down by sorrowful recollections, begins to sense renewed purpose. He sees that the memory of past misses can sharpen his resolve to seize present openings. An orchard might no longer remain as it was, but other adventures await if he dares to claim them. Each time he transforms a regret into constructive activity, he breaks the pattern of shame and inertia.

This journey does not produce overnight miracles. Felix still feels twinges of regret. Some nights, old memories resurface, but now he wields tools to address them. Apologies, new goals, self-forgiveness, acceptance of the unchangeable, and honest reflection all combine to keep him on a productive path. He realises he is learning to live with regret, not in it. As time passes, the regrets lose their sharpness, replaced by a growing sense that he is finally making amends, if only by refusing to repeat the same mistakes.

Whether this transformation lasts until the end of his sixth life rests on his consistency. Regret will always linger in some form, but if Felix remains proactive, the final pages of this life might be written with hope, not sorrow. You can view his steps as a framework for tackling your own regrets: clarify them, address them one by one, set forward goals, practise self-forgiveness, accept what cannot be changed, and keep watch so regret does not creep in anew. This shift can turn a life overshadowed by loss into one guided by redemption.

Conclusion of Sixth Life

Felix's sixth life, shaped by regret, reveals how haunting old sorrows can freeze you in place, draining excitement from each dawn. Missed opportunities, recalled in painful detail, can overshadow any new possibilities if you let them. Yet this chapter also shows that regret need not remain a purely destructive force. It becomes toxic only when allowed to stifle growth. If you are willing to examine your regrets without sinking into despair, they can become signposts for what truly matters.

By exploring the root causes and effects of regret, Felix gradually realises that his remorse signifies how deeply he values certain experiences and relationships. That revelation can spur him toward better habits, fresh attempts, and redemption wherever possible. Although the past remains sealed, the future still stands open. Each day offers a choice: dwell on what might have been or transform those pangs of loss into a catalyst for action.

If Felix stays the course, he may find that a life once weighed down by remorse can still flower into something meaningful, fuelled by lessons learned through pain. Regret then ceases to be a chain and becomes a reminder to embrace the present wholeheartedly. This chapter invites you to do the same. Ask yourself which regrets stalk your own path and whether you can redirect their energy toward constructive change. Doing so requires courage, honesty, and perseverance but can prevent regret from claiming another chapter of your life. The clock still ticks for Felix; hopefully, he will harness his regrets as a final wake-up call, forging a future less governed by sorrow and more lit by a determination to do better, one choice at a time.

The Seventh Life

Distraction

You might think that after regret, Felix would live this new life with sharper focus than ever before. Having learned the sting of missed opportunities, he should be prepared to commit wholeheartedly to his goals. Yet a different obstacle emerges: distraction. Felix discovers that instead of ignoring his regrets, he now scurries from one novelty to the next, never lingering long enough to achieve genuine progress. This seventh life becomes a restless dance from fleeting thrill to fleeting thrill.

Distraction looks harmless on the surface; in fact, it can feel like relief. Each time Felix feels a twinge of boredom or an echo of old remorse, something new beckons. Perhaps it is a playful mouse, a social event, a sunny rooftop, or a passing shadow that demands investigation. Before he realises it, the day vanishes in a blur of half-done tasks and shallow connections. While fear or regret once paralysed him, distraction scatters his energy in countless directions.

This chapter explores how distraction thwarts you from diving deeply into tasks or relationships. Through five subheadings, you will see how Felix's attention frays, why endless novelty seems so seductive, how the root causes of distraction hide beneath surface-level amusements, which philosophical teachings address scattered living, and what practical methods might help Felix reclaim his focus. As you read, you may notice your own life's diversions, times when one more scroll, one more chat, or one more minor task sabotaged bigger dreams.

Can Felix break free of this seventh snare and harness the continuity needed to leave a real mark on the world? Or will the gentle pull of a million small diversions lure him toward another life wasted? You may recognise your own internal tug-of-war here, making Felix's new struggle both familiar and urgent.

A Thousand Shiny Distractions

Imagine Felix waking in this seventh life with a sense of renewed possibility. After grappling with regret, he feels determined not to let opportunities slip by again. However, unlike in his sixth life, he does not brood on the past. Instead, he leaps toward any interesting sound or sight as if the mere act of constant motion might save him from regret's shadow. When a friend meows about a new hideout, he dashes off to see it; if a dog barks, he rushes away to investigate or flee. He never stays in one place for more than a short time.

At first, this seems like progress. Felix is no longer stuck in sorrow. He is active, social, and engaged. Yet a pattern emerges: every fresh invitation or curiosity claims his attention, pulling him away from tasks he has barely begun. If he starts hunting to sharpen his skills, a sudden noise distracts him; he drops the hunt to chase a leaf blowing across the path. When he tries forging alliances with neighbouring cats, some minor drama in another alley draws him off before he can cement any real bond. By the end of each day, his to-do list remains half-finished and scattered.

You may recall moments in your own life where you felt a flicker of ambition but found yourself checking trivial updates, drifting through quick social exchanges, or starting projects that never advanced past the opening stage. Distraction is not always loud or forceful; it often creeps in quietly, offering small pleasures or fleeting engagement. Over time, it chips away at depth and continuity. Felix experiences this constantly, leaping from novelty to novelty, telling himself he will return to each task "in a moment," though that moment seldom arrives.

Socially, Felix's new acquaintances find him entertaining, initially. He appears at gatherings, trades bits of gossip, and then vanishes. He flirts with friendships but never invests in the trust or shared experiences that breed real closeness. Even those who like him wonder why he never settles to have a meaningful conversation. Before any topic grows profound, Felix's gaze drifts away to something else that stirs his curiosity. This fosters a reputation for being charming but unreliable.

Further, distraction saps the joy of deeper accomplishment. Felix once longed to master a skill or make a tangible difference. Now, he flits through so many minor pursuits that each one remains superficial. He might chase a butterfly for a few moments, then spy a group of cats playing near a bin and dash over to join them, only to abandon them mid-game when a stray noise invites him elsewhere. Each diversion is pleasant for an instant, yet he ends many days feeling strangely hollow.

On a broader level, distraction clouds self-awareness. Because Felix rarely lingers with his own thoughts, he seldom reflects on what he truly desires or which direction is worth long-term commitment. Whenever a whisper of introspection tries to surface, the next sparkly event in the environment captures his focus. You may have experienced something akin to this: each time you think about your deeper purpose, a phone buzz or a trivial chore derails that train of thought. Over weeks and months, it becomes a habit to avoid prolonged reflection.

In some ways, distraction can be an unconscious strategy to evade regret or fear. Felix senses, at the edges of his mind, the guilt and shame from previous mistakes. Rather than allowing those emotions to guide him toward growth, he floods his attention with busy trifles, ensuring there is no mental space to dwell on pain. This short-term relief has a long-term cost: unprocessed feelings remain unhealed, lurking beneath a swirl of shallow activities.

Meanwhile, tangible goals slip away. If Felix once planned to be a stronger hunter, share knowledge with new friends, or explore challenging territories, these ambitions falter in the face of endless small diversions. Each day ends with him realising he has not advanced an inch toward the bigger aims he once held. Distraction, in that sense, acts like a slow leak in a boat: while he is chasing minor amusements, valuable time drains away.

To an outside observer, Felix seems lively, always on the move. Yet if you watch closely, you see no direction in that movement, no underlying continuity. It is all reaction, no sustained action. If you have felt similarly, you know how easy it is to mistake busyness for productivity or social hopping for meaningful relationships. By scattering your attention among countless minor tasks and interactions, you never anchor yourself deeply in any single pursuit.

In short, Felix's world is full of "shiny objects" calling his name. None of them is inherently harmful. The real issue is that each new pull on his attention interrupts and displaces the last. While fear or regret once pinned him down, distraction lightly but persistently tugs him away from focus. The result can be another life wasted, albeit in a seemingly cheerful flurry of partial engagements.

The only question is whether Felix will notice that his days are peppered with hollow progress. After a while, he might detect the pattern of beginnings with no endings, promising starts with no follow-through. That moment of realisation can be pivotal: either he becomes aware that distraction is diluting his potential, or he remains enthralled by the swirl of tempting trifles. For now, he keeps bounding from one interesting scene to the next, convinced he is living vibrantly yet inadvertently avoiding any venture that requires sustained concentration.

Why Distraction Feels So Appealing

If you have ever attempted a demanding task, you know how a small diversion, like a quick break or a social media glance, can be surprisingly tempting. The same is true for Felix, who finds each sudden noise or fleeting encounter irresistibly fresh. Understanding why distraction appeals so strongly might help both you and Felix see how it can hijack progress.

A key factor is the brain's craving for novelty. Research shows that new stimuli can trigger reward mechanisms, releasing tiny sparks of pleasure or curiosity. In feline terms, every fluttering leaf or unknown alley piques Felix's interest. Repetitive effort, such as honing a skill or forging deeper connections, demands patience. By contrast, a brand-new stimulus offers immediate excitement, however brief. Felix's mind, like yours, can become hooked on that novelty buzz, leaping from one interesting thing to the next to sustain a steady flow of minor thrills.

Another driving force is the desire to avoid discomfort. True growth often requires facing dull practice sessions, uncertain outcomes, or emotional self-examination. Distraction offers an easy way out: instead of pushing through that discomfort, Felix diverts his focus to something less taxing. This pattern is common among humans who procrastinate on big projects, drawn to simple amusements that spare them from the strain or fear of failure. Felix, though not procrastinating in the old sense, uses minor amusements to dodge the deeper effort that lasting accomplishment demands.

Moreover, the fear of missing out can feed distraction. Felix sees a group of cats gathering for a lively chase, so he abandons his solitary hunting practice to join them, worried that he might lose an enjoyable moment. Another day, a rumour surfaces about a hidden stash of food, so he drops his attempts at building alliances to chase that rumour. By chasing everything, he ends up missing the benefits of a single, focused pursuit. You might recall times in your own life where multiple intriguing invitations made you flit around, ultimately achieving little.

Social validation also plays a role. Felix has discovered that bouncing between groups makes him appear energetic and popular, at least at first glance. Each new set of acquaintances sees him as that sociable cat who appears in their alley, adding a spark of novelty to their routine. Yet this fleeting popularity rarely matures into genuine trust since Felix never stays long enough to prove himself reliable. Still,

Distraction

the immediate feedback loop, friendly greetings and admiration for his lively presence can be addictive.

Additionally, the modern environment (or, in Felix's case, a world teeming with new sights and sounds) fosters shorter attention spans. When stimuli abound, moving from one highlight to the next feels natural. If you live among constant pings, alerts, or shifting visuals, you might mirror Felix's restlessness, finding it harder to remain immersed in one task for an extended period. Even in a cat's reality, the ever-changing hustle of city life can undermine the will to focus.

Past experiences can also reinforce distraction. Felix, for instance, left behind a life of regret and sorrow. Quick diversions act like a shield against the deeper emotional labour of introspection. Each time a memory of regret threatens to surface, a new excitement or minor mission distracts him, preventing painful reflection. He rationalises that perpetual motion is better than wallowing, not realising he sacrifices depth and continuity in the process.

Another subtle cause is the erosion of personal priorities. If Felix lacks a defined sense of which goals or relationships matter most, he is susceptible to every beckoning impulse. In your own life, you might have found that clarity of purpose helps you resist distractions; when you know exactly what you need to do, fleeting attractions lose power. Felix, on the other hand, has only a vague resolve to avoid regret, but no concrete plan to make the most of his seventh life. This vacuum of priorities leaves him open to anything that glitters in the moment.

In summary, distraction's appeal arises from novelty, comfort, avoiding deeper challenges, social praise, environmental stimuli, and the absence of a strong internal compass. Combine these factors, and you have a potent recipe for scattered attention. Each small attraction feels harmless, even beneficial, yet collectively they siphon the time and energy needed for meaningful undertakings. Felix remains in a perpetual state of partial engagement, never fully present or committed to a single path.

Understanding these roots is vital if Felix hopes to reclaim his focus. Merely berating himself for being "too distracted" will not suffice; he needs to see why each diversion exerts such a pull, so he can approach it more consciously. You might do the same in your own struggles with scattered attention, pausing to ask: "What am I escaping by diving into this trivial novelty? What deeper effort am I sidestepping?" This self-inquiry can begin to dismantle distraction's charm and redirect you toward sustained growth.

The Cost of Fragmented Attention

Distraction is often framed as a simple quirk or minor failing, yet its real cost can be profound. For Felix, the seventh life might slip away in shallow pursuits if he does not recognise how fragmented attention undermines everything he attempts. Likewise, you may discover that scattered focus quietly drains motivation, relationships, and real progress, leaving only a series of partial experiences and incomplete outcomes.

One immediate toll is the decline in skill mastery. Felix once hoped to refine his hunting techniques or help younger cats, but every time he begins, a new curiosity beckons him away.

Consequently, he never achieves the repetitive practice or immersive involvement required to excel. He remains at a basic level, incapable of advanced hunts or coherent mentoring. It is not that he lacks talent; he lacks sustained concentration. You might relate if you have ever tried to learn an instrument, a language, or any complex task while constantly multi-tasking and switching your attention.

Social bonds also suffer. True companionship emerges from shared experiences, vulnerability, and time spent delving beyond polite small talk. Felix, bouncing from cat to cat, only skims the surface of each potential friendship. He might be well-known in passing, but no one truly relies on him. Over time, this fosters a sense of loneliness, ironically under a veneer of social busyness. If you have drifted through gatherings without forging deeper connections, you understand how easy it is to appear sociable yet remain emotionally distant.

Another cost is the stunting of creativity. Felix occasionally has sparks of invention or new ideas, but never sits still long enough to explore them. Original thinking often arises when you focus on a question or problem for an extended period. Fragmented attention disrupts that mental continuity, so insights remain half-formed. You might find that your best breakthroughs occur after you concentrate on a challenge, letting your mind roam within a single context. Distraction disrupts that process, leaving potential discoveries unexplored.

Emotional resilience declines as well. Felix rarely processes his own feelings thoroughly, skipping from one external stimulus to the next. When a minor setback occurs, like failing to catch prey or losing a small item, he lacks the emotional bandwidth to handle frustration. Instead, he rushes into the next distraction, never developing the capacity to cope with adversity. Over time, this undermines confidence and fosters an avoidant mindset: a single negative experience can derail him if he has not cultivated patience and emotional fortitude.

Furthermore, Felix loses track of time. Days blur when each hour is filled with scattered mini-tasks or fleeting amusements. He might intend to dedicate a morning to building alliances, only to realise midday that he has roamed off to chase random noises. The day ends with little to show, and the pattern repeats. If you have experienced constant interruption, you know how entire weeks can vanish in a haze of half-finished pursuits, leaving you wondering where your time went.

On a broader scale, distraction erodes self-respect. Each dawn, Felix might vow to accomplish specific goals, but by dusk, he has flitted around without completing anything substantial. These daily letdowns chip away at his confidence. He begins to see himself as scattered, unreliable, and incapable of follow-through, which can become a self-fulfilling prophecy. You might have felt similarly if repeated attempts to focus repeatedly collapsed under trivial diversions.

Another invisible cost is that Felix fails to capitalise on synergy. Tasks or projects often gain momentum when built upon day after day. Imagine if Felix decided to assist new kittens every morning: each session would build trust, knowledge, and routine. Distraction interrupts that accumulation, resetting him to square one each time. He never reaches the point where efforts compound, reaping greater rewards over the long run. This absence of consistent momentum can render even the best-intentioned plans futile.

Finally, fragmented attention can block the satisfaction of being fully present. When you immerse yourself in a worthy activity, you experience a flow state: time may pass swiftly, yet the sense of fulfilment is deep. Felix seldom attains that flow, because his mind leaps from one lure to the next before any deeper engagement can blossom. The day's experiences remain disjointed, each overshadowed by whatever caught his eye next. Over time, he recognises a persistent superficiality in all he does.

Hence, the cost of distraction is not a small inconvenience; it is the slow dissolution of potential. Felix, if he does not correct this course, will find his seventh life scattered and inconsequential. Instead of forging achievements or bonds that endure, he will collect trivial memories of flitting here and there. In your own context, you might see how recurring diversions have consumed hours or months that could have fostered true progress or heartfelt connections.

This realisation might jolt Felix awake at some point. Perhaps an old friend highlights his inconstancy, or he notices that younger cats he meant to guide have advanced without him. If so, he might see that the swirling web of small amusements has robbed him of the depth he once longed for. Recognising the cost is the first step toward resisting distraction's pull. Without that recognition, he stands poised to let another life vanish in a flurry of inconsequential events, never harnessing the power of sustained focus.

Philosophical Perspectives on Distraction

Though the world of a cat may seem distant from human society, the challenge of distraction resonates across times and cultures. Philosophers have long considered how scattered attention derails personal growth, creativity, and even moral integrity. By revisiting these insights, Felix could gain a roadmap for recapturing the discipline that endless novelty tends to erode.

Stoic thought suggests that external events, including random appeals to your senses, should not govern you. Instead, your focus ought to be grounded in reasoned intent. If Felix adopted this stance, he would filter each stimulus through a deliberate lens: "Does this help my overarching goal, or is it merely pulling me off track?" This self-questioning might shield him from the passive compliance that currently scatters his energy.

Meanwhile, certain Buddhist teachings highlight mindfulness: being present in each moment without letting the mind wander. In essence, if you root your awareness firmly, you become less vulnerable to distractions. Felix could practise pausing whenever a new noise or social happening arises, asking himself whether it aligns with his deeper purpose before reacting. Rather than drifting mindlessly, he would respond with clear judgment about whether the diversion genuinely matters.

Existential philosophy underscores the freedom, and responsibility, you have in choosing your path. By default, you might sink into distraction because it is easier than grappling with meaningful choices. Yet existential thinkers warn that fleeing from self-directed purpose into scattered busyness robs life of authentic substance. If Felix truly values his independence, he must guard that freedom by not allowing every trivial impulse to steer him.

From a different angle, certain Taoist ideas suggest that living in harmony with a natural flow involves mindful engagement. Some might confuse that concept with letting yourself be carried by every passing current. However, genuine Taoist thinking posits that alignment arises when you act from a balanced centre, not from random impulses. Felix's hectic chasing of stimuli is the opposite of calm awareness; he is not living fluidly, but fractiously.

Other philosophical schools emphasise moderation and structured routine. For instance, Aristotelian thought speaks of virtues cultivated through habitual practice. Distraction undermines that practice by preventing the consistent repetition needed to build character or skill. If Felix fails to remain steady in any pursuit, he stifles the cultivation of excellence. He might think he is broadening his experience, but in truth, he is skimming the surface of life without deepening any virtue.

On a spiritual level, many traditions assert that inner stillness fosters clarity and genuine wisdom. The frantic swirl of distractions keeps Felix forever outward-focused, preventing the introspection that leads to personal transformation. By spending time in quiet reflection, or even structured solitude, he might see through the lure of trivial amusements and reconnect with a more profound sense of purpose.

Philosophers also warn of how distraction erodes moral judgment. When you flit from impulse to impulse, you rarely pause to weigh the ethical implications. Felix may inadvertently let down friends or abandon responsibilities simply because something momentarily more interesting appears. Over time, such small lapses accumulate, harming his integrity and the trust others place in him. A cat guided by fleeting impulses might easily cross boundaries he never intended to violate, all for the sake of novelty.

Furthermore, certain Stoic and Buddhist texts caution that untrained attention leads to suffering. Your mind becomes restless, never content, always seeking the next stimulation. This restlessness can breed anxiety, as you fear missing out on something better elsewhere, perpetuating a cycle of dissatisfaction. Felix, convinced he is enjoying maximum freedom, might actually be ensnared by the compulsion to chase everything, never finding peace or deeper fulfilment.

Taken together, these philosophical insights urge deliberate, conscious engagement. Rather than letting circumstances yank your mind around, you maintain control by setting intentions, practising consistent habits, and fostering an inner calm that can resist each ephemeral allure. For Felix, adopting these methods would mean stepping back from the swirl of daily enticements and re-establishing priorities, forging routines that reflect what he deems truly worthwhile.

Whether he can do so depends on his willingness to face the uneasy truth that his scattered approach has a high cost. The user-friendly convenience of constant novelty blinds him to the need for reflection and discipline. He may have to consciously limit certain amusements or designate time for solitary focus. In short, he must adopt a measure of restraint and structure, concepts that have guided wise living for millennia. The final question is whether he will gather the resolve to implement them.

Rekindling Depth and Focus

Distraction

Eventually, Felix's restless escapades grow repetitive. He begins to realise how each day ends with the same hollow sense of having accomplished nothing lasting. This fatigue with trivial novelty can become the pivot point toward real change. You might have felt a similar moment: the instant you see that flitting between distractions yields only fragments of satisfaction, prompting you to search for a deeper path.

The first step is clarifying purpose. Felix sits in a quiet alley one evening, acknowledging that his life is draining away in scattered pursuits. He recalls how in earlier lives, a touch of direction, like helping kittens or mastering a skill, gave him a reason to wake with energy. Now, he sets a simple but concrete goal. Perhaps he decides to thoroughly explore a distant section of the neighbourhood, forging lasting alliances there. In writing or in your mind, you could do the same, naming a mission that genuinely matters to you.

Next, Felix commits to a small daily routine that aligns with his goal. If, for instance, he aims to become a reliable guide for younger cats, he dedicates a portion of each morning to meeting them at a known spot, teaching them essential survival methods. Even if a bigger distraction calls, he trains himself to return to that session. Over time, this consistent effort begins building deeper bonds and skills. The repetitive continuity fosters mastery and reliability. You might replicate this approach in your own life by scheduling a fixed window to practise, learn, or connect more meaningfully.

Of course, distractions still beckon. Felix handles this by training his reaction. When a minor noise or passing cat tries to pull him away, he pauses and asks, "Does this serve my current priority?" If the answer is no, he acknowledges the temptation but chooses to remain on task. This habit of pausing short-circuits the automatic impulse that once had him bounding off. You might use a similar technique, whether it is turning off extra notifications or politely declining invitations that do not align with your primary objective.

Additionally, Felix gives himself time for fun but structures it. Instead of letting amusements intrude whenever they wish, he designates periods for roaming freely. By reserving that space, he keeps the rest of his schedule clear for purposeful activity. This balance ensures he does not become rigid or joyless, but neither does he revert to constant fragmentation. If you have tried this, you know how scheduling specific breaks can preserve your momentum while still granting leisure.

Another crucial element is reflection. At day's end, Felix quickly reviews how he spent his hours. Did he remain faithful to his chosen focus? If distractions pulled him off course, how can he handle them better tomorrow? This gentle self-check fosters accountability without harshness, letting him adjust course before small diversions morph into a return to scattered living. You might do something similar, making it part of a nightly routine to note successes and snags in your quest for deeper engagement.

Felix also learns the value of single-tasking. When he decides to assist younger cats, he immerses himself fully, ignoring other background stimuli. Initially, this feels uncomfortable, he wonders what he might be missing. Yet as he persists, he discovers the satisfaction of truly connecting with them, seeing their progress, and finishing a session with tangible results. This sense of closure and impact replaces the flighty

Distraction

rush of new amusements, giving him a more solid sense of achievement.

Handling social dynamics also matters. Felix is used to drifting among different groups, but now he invests in fewer but more meaningful relationships. He chooses a circle of cats who share his aspiration or at least respect his focus. When trivial drama flares, he politely excuses himself if it jeopardises his commitments. Over time, real trust grows, as these cats see Felix's consistent presence and dedication. You might mirror this by selectively deepening certain friendships, rather than spreading your attention too thin.

A pivotal shift occurs when Felix realises that fewer, well-chosen pursuits yield more genuine joy than a hundred shallow forays. Whether he is learning an advanced hunting trick, guiding a cat who is new to the area, or simply forging a stable routine, he feels a depth of satisfaction unknown in the swirl of random diversions. This realisation cements his resolve, helping him brush aside fresh temptations with greater ease.

Finally, Felix acknowledges that the urge to chase novelty never fully disappears. At times, a friend's casual remark about a new gathering might tempt him away. Instead of demonising that impulse, he recognises it as part of his nature: curiosity is good, but unchecked curiosity leads to chaos. By blending curiosity with discipline, he shapes a life that balances discovery and focus. You might do the same by allowing yourself spontaneous indulgences within reasonable limits, ensuring they do not sabotage your main priorities.

Through these steps, clarifying purpose, building routines, pausing before impulse, single-tasking, selective social bonds, and mindful acceptance of curiosity, Felix discovers that the seventh life can avoid the fate of scattered inconsequence. He reclaims the ability to finish what he starts and form authentic connections. Each morning greets him not with an endless buffet of trivial amusements, but with a smaller set of chosen tasks he approaches wholeheartedly. The result is a slower pace but far deeper living.

Whether this transformation endures until the end of his seventh life depends on his consistency. Distraction always waits in the wings, ready to pounce whenever he grows complacent or bored. Yet if Felix stands firm, guided by the lessons of older lives and the philosophical wisdom that shaped his resolve, he may finally see that sustained attention opens the door to profound achievements and relationships. In your own struggle with distraction, you might find a reflection of these same truths: depth arises when you filter out the noise and give yourself fully to the tasks and connections that truly matter.

Conclusion of Seventh Life

Felix's seventh life illustrates that not all obstacles come as fear or regret. Sometimes, the biggest threat is the allure of endless distractions. On the surface, flitting from one novelty to another seems lively. In reality, it quickly unravels any hope of continuity or achievement. Days go by in a flurry of activity, yet no deep bonds or significant goals take shape. The seductive call of "what's next?" overshadows the power of sustained engagement.

Distraction

Through examining the roots and consequences of distraction, Felix realises how easily fleeting impulses eclipse lasting purpose. This chapter shows that without mindful structure, meaningful tasks remain half-done and relationships never mature beyond casual acquaintance. Philosophical teachings, from Stoicism to mindfulness, propose methods to remain focused, urging you to pause before leaping onto every new sparkly path.

When Felix eventually confronts the emptiness of scattered attention, he begins forging a more deliberate life. By selecting a guiding goal, practising small routines, and filtering out aimless appeals, he finds greater satisfaction in fewer, more valued pursuits. This deliberate stance frees him from chasing every glimmer that crosses his path. In shifting from shallow busyness to depth of purpose, he escapes the risk of another wasted existence.

In your own world, the lesson stands clear: if you constantly let your attention fragment, you lose the chance to cultivate real mastery, closeness, or personal growth. Distraction seldom arrives as a roaring beast; it drips into your routine as innocent diversions, gradually eroding momentum. Like Felix, you can awake to this pattern, adopt strategies to guard your focus, and rediscover the steady fulfilment that emerges when you give your best attention to what matters most.

The Eighth Life

Mediocrity

You have followed Felix through seven distinct lives, watching him battle fear, drift in comfort, procrastinate, chase approval, wander aimlessly, wrestle with regret, and scatter his focus amid distraction. Each time, he found a lesson, though always later than hoped. Now, at the dawn of his eighth life, Felix encounters a more insidious challenge: the life of mediocrity. Rather than being visibly trapped or haunted, he slips into a steady existence of "good enough," never demanding excellence from himself or his circumstances.

This eighth life feels calm at first. Felix faces no deep fears; he no longer flits about in wild distractions. He shows up to daily tasks, forging mild friendships and achieving basic goals. On the surface, there is nothing especially wrong. Yet a persistent sense of dissatisfaction lurks beneath the quiet routine. Felix suspects he was meant for more but lacks the drive to go beyond the ordinary.

In this chapter, you will see how mediocrity can lull you into thinking you are doing fine while stealing your potential for greatness. Through five subheadings, you will explore how Felix's aim for "adequate" keeps him from pushing boundaries, how it dulls ambition, why it might feel safer than striving, and which philosophical insights call for rejecting average. Ultimately, you will learn practical ways to break free from the comfort of middle ground, turning your eighth life, or your own journey, into something more extraordinary.

Mediocrity

Does Felix awaken to the subtle losses inflicted by mediocrity, or will he slip toward a quiet, grey conclusion, never discovering the heights he could have scaled? As you read, you may glimpse your own moments of settling for "enough" instead of going all in. The question is whether you will, like Felix, sense the deeper calling that demands you rise above the merely passable.

The Comfort of the Ordinary

Imagine Felix beginning his eighth life with a cautious optimism. He is free from crippling fear, no longer scuttling after distractions, and not particularly haunted by regret. He sets out each day with mild intentions, catching enough food to stay fed, mingling enough with other cats to avoid loneliness. Everything he does is sufficient, but never outstanding. Though he retains faint memories of past mistakes and unfulfilled ambitions, he chooses the middle path, safe, predictable, and unthreatening.

This ordinary path offers a soothing stability. Felix experiences neither the drama of past extremes nor the emptiness of wandering. Instead, he finds moderate success in hunting, forms polite acquaintances, and keeps a tidy routine. If you watched from the sidelines, you might say Felix seems "balanced." Yet, beneath that veneer, he has quietly abandoned anything that might demand serious risk or innovation. By steering clear of bold goals, he also sidesteps the possibility of falling short.

You might recognise this pull in your own life. After enduring stress or upheaval, mediocrity feels like a haven. It promises no harsh failures, no exhausting drives, no endless regrets. Why chase excellence when "just fine" spares you from disappointment? Felix embraces this mindset. But as the days pass, he notices a dullness creeping in. He sees other cats displaying bursts of creativity or forging remarkable alliances. He wonders if they face greater challenges but also reap richer rewards.

Socially, mediocrity cements a modest reputation for Felix. No one praises him as a leader or visionary, yet no one scorns him as lazy or chaotic. He floats along in a grey zone, well-liked but unexceptional. The circle of cats around him reflect the same mindset, friendly, agreeable, and content to stay within the familiar. At times, Felix senses a restlessness, a desire to aim higher, but he hushes that impulse, convinced that stepping beyond average is too risky.

In practical terms, settling for ordinary means Felix rarely improves upon his baseline skills. His hunts remain serviceable but never advanced. His social ties remain cordial but never profound. He avoids forging any big plans that might push him to learn, adapt, or sacrifice. From the outside, he appears stable, but internally, he drifts toward stagnation. You might have felt this drift as well, a period when you survived competently, yet felt no spark driving you to excel.

One subtle appeal of mediocrity is the applause of common approval. Many cats appreciate Felix's non-threatening, steady presence. He does not ruffle fur with grand ambitions or criticism of the status quo. Because he upholds the everyday norms, no one questions him, and no one challenges him to do more. This acceptance can be pleasant, offering a sense of belonging that is not tinged with jealousy or contention. But it also discourages him from exploring bold paths.

Mediocrity

Mediocrity also fosters a reluctance to take risks. If Felix contemplated a more challenging hunt or a bigger territorial claim, the possibility of failure looms. Why venture into a new area where he might fail, when the current situation is tolerable? Fear of failure, no longer a constant shadow, reappears in subtle forms. Rather than making him hide, it nudges him to remain in the safe bounds of "okay." Ambition, once a motivator, shrinks under the weight of "Why fix what isn't broken?"

The cost of this mindset soon surfaces. Felix realises that while life flows smoothly, he feels no surge of pride or excitement. Each morning merges into the next with a dull predictability. Tasks, hunts, and social visits become rote. He experiences neither deep lows nor thrilling highs. It is a life free from major pain but also devoid of the profound joys that come from pushing limits. When he sees cats around him occasionally achieving something remarkable, he experiences a vague envy mixed with resignation, an unspoken sense that excellence is for others.

Over time, mediocrity also shrinks his sense of possibility. Initially, Felix might have considered stepping up to lead a small group of cats to a better territory. But the more he remains in average routines, the more those ideas feel distant. He no longer sees himself as capable of major feats. The boundaries of what is possible narrow, governed by the mundane successes he repeats each day. You might notice a similar effect: the longer you stay in your comfort zone, the more daunting it becomes to leave.

In social settings, Felix's relationships lack depth and challenge. True friendships often flourish when you tackle shared problems or celebrate each other's breakthroughs. By avoiding large endeavours, Felix robs himself of the camaraderie that emerges from striving alongside others. Friendships remain mild and stable, but never transformative. There are few stories to recount, few memories of triumph or growth, only a gentle, ongoing routine that fosters shallow bonds.

Thus, the comfort of the ordinary wields a double-edged sword. It protects Felix from heartbreak and extreme disappointments, yet it also lulls him into a half-engaged existence. He never experiences the intense satisfaction of conquering a new height, forging a powerful alliance, or mastering a skill to near-perfection. Everything is "all right," but nothing sparkles. The question is whether Felix will notice this creeping dullness before his eighth life closes. Mediocrity, while unchallenging, can swiftly transform into regret if left unexamined.

Why We Settle for Less

If you reflect on Felix's journey, you might ask, "After so many lessons, why would he settle for mediocrity instead of striving for greatness?" The reasons are woven from relief, fear, and a misunderstanding of what it means to thrive. Many of these motives mirror our own impulses. Understanding them can clarify why any of us might choose the middle ground over excellence.

First, mediocrity serves as a refuge from the turmoil of previous mistakes. Felix remembers how fear nearly paralysed him, how regret tormented him, and how distractions led him astray. Mediocrity, by contrast, promises fewer emotional ups and downs. It whispers, "Stay in safe waters, and you will not drown." This avoidance strategy underpins much of his contentment with average outcomes. He is tired of drama and welcomes the calm of settling for less.

Second, stepping beyond mediocrity demands sustained effort. Felix has glimpsed how lofty goals require daily discipline, risk-taking, and the possibility of visible failure. Compared to that, mediocre achievements are straightforward and low-risk. He needs only maintain the routine he has established, never venturing too far. This minimal-effort approach might not excite him, but it also does not scare him. You may have felt a similar pull: the path of least resistance often seems the simplest route to steady comfort.

Third, Felix confuses a lack of glaring problems with genuine happiness. In earlier lives, he dealt with clear crises, crippling fear, painful regret, or aimless distraction. Now, none of those spectres loom. He mistakes the absence of negativity for the presence of real fulfilment. This confusion leads him to assume he is doing fine, never probing whether "fine" is truly the best he can do. You might have felt this if you have ever drifted in a mediocre job or relationship simply because it was not blatantly terrible.

Another factor is the sense of belonging that mediocrity can foster. Felix's unremarkable lifestyle meshes seamlessly with many of the cats around him, who also prefer the steady and predictable. If he strove for something bigger, he might stand out or lose favour among those who resent or envy ambition. Remaining average keeps him in the comfortable majority. On a human level, you might have experienced social pressure to stay at the same level as peers, fearing that chasing excellence could isolate you.

Additionally, Felix might be recovering from regret, reluctant to invest heavily in a project that could backfire and leave him bruised by remorse once more. By aiming moderately, he minimises the emotional risk. If he never dreams too big, he never has to confront the pain of a shattered goal. But this also means he forfeits the chance to triumph in ways that feed the soul. The correlation between fear of regret and settling for less is strong: disappointment in the past can weaken one's desire to try wholeheartedly again.

Another subtle reason involves limited self-belief. While Felix has overcome some old patterns, he has yet to experience consistent success that might boost his confidence. In this eighth life, he might view himself as someone destined to be mediocre because of all the near-misses and mild outcomes in prior incarnations. Without a track record of excellence, he presumes it is not in his nature. You might identify with this if repeated average results lead you to conclude you are not capable of pushing higher, ignoring the possibility that your environment or mindset held you back.

Finally, there is a cultural element: the local cat community might have norms that favour unambitious living. Perhaps they see big dreams as impractical or self-indulgent. In your own world, you might have grown up in an environment that discouraged too much "showing off." Mediocrity can become a silent agreement not to strive too far, as that could disrupt the social fabric. Felix, unwilling to rock the boat, falls neatly into line.

All these factors converge to make mediocrity look appealing. He avoids the spikes of stress and disappointment that haunted him in earlier lives, nestles into a pleasant routine, and garners easy acceptance from the group. Yet, as you will see in the next sections, the price of this safe harbour is the slow suffocation of any extraordinary potential. Felix will need a spark, perhaps an encounter or a realisation, to awaken him to how limiting "just enough" can be. If he continues to settle, he may one day confront a final regret: that he had the capacity for much more, but never dared to demand it.

The Unseen Cost of Living Below Potential

On the surface, Felix's eighth life seems comfortable enough. He greets each dawn without dread, interacts amiably with fellow cats, and ends his evenings satisfied that he did "enough" to get by. No dramatic conflicts or heartbreak riddle his days. Yet as the weeks roll on, a quiet itch grows, warning him that existing below his potential exacts a subtle but profound toll.

One immediate cost is the atrophy of ambition. If you do not exercise your drive to improve, it fades like an unused muscle. Each time Felix opts for the easiest route, he weakens his capacity for challenge. Instead of building confidence through tackling hard goals, he teaches himself that "good enough" suffices. Over time, the very notion of pushing harder becomes foreign, draining any spark that might have led him to excel.

Another consequence is the underdevelopment of skills and talents. Felix might have a knack for strategic hunting or be a natural leader in group endeavours. But mediocrity prevents him from testing those strengths in challenging situations. He never invests the time to refine or expand his capabilities, leaving them dormant. In human terms, it is like having a latent gift for music, but only ever playing a few simple tunes, never delving deeper to see what you could truly achieve.

Socially, mediocre living also limits his influence. If Felix settled for average, no one sees him as a resource for significant undertakings or a source of inspiring leadership. He remains a pleasant background presence, never the cat others rally around when a bigger project arises. This feeds a cycle: because he never steps up, no one expects him to, reinforcing his sense that it is not his place to aim high. You might have observed a similar dynamic: once you get pegged as "unremarkable," opportunities for real impact rarely come your way.

Emotionally, living below potential fosters a kind of muted dissatisfaction. Felix cannot point to anything obviously wrong, but he feels a lingering sense of being unfulfilled. Each day's routine meets basic needs yet fails to ignite real passion. That mild restlessness occasionally surfaces as envy when he sees other cats truly excel. In your life, you might recall times when you watched someone shine in a field you once dreamed of pursuing, feeling both happy for them and a pang of regret for yourself.

This subdued existence also hampers creativity. The drive to innovate or explore usually arises when you stretch beyond your comfort zone. Felix, opting for safe hunts and routine paths, rarely stumbles upon novel solutions or fresh insights. His daily life repeats set patterns, leaving little room for experimentation. If you have ever felt that your imagination flourishes only when you challenge yourself, you understand how mediocrity starves creative impulses.

Another silent cost is the erosion of deeper connections. True camaraderie can blossom in adversity or in pursuit of a shared grand aim. Felix's mild relationships remain on the safe side, never tested by joint ambitions or supportive leaps

Mediocrity

of faith. Without those forging experiences, the bonds stay surface-level. The intimacy that arises from facing challenges together never fully develops. Mediocrity thus deprives Felix of the potential for transformative friendships.

Furthermore, mediocrity can slip into long-term regret. Though Felix's earlier lives taught him regret is painful, he has not yet realised that coasting might set him up for a final wave of disappointment near life's end. If he later glances back and sees he never aspired beyond the mundane, that sting could be as sharp as any heartbreak. The notion that he consistently chose "okay" instead of discovering his true limits might overshadow any short-term relief gained by playing it safe.

A final aspect is how mediocrity blocks the broader positive influence Felix might have in his community. Even a single cat's push for excellence can inspire others or solve collective problems. By settling, Felix deprives the neighbourhood of what his best efforts could have contributed, whether that is improved security, knowledge, or unity. This unfulfilled communal role remains invisible as long as he quietly does "just enough."

In short, living below potential reaps no immediate crisis but exacts a hefty price in lost ambition, unsharpened skills, shallow relationships, stifled creativity, and potential regret. Felix, though stable, starts sensing a growing unease as each day passes without challenge or growth. He may not yet label it as "the cost of mediocrity," but the signs emerge in his subdued emotions and fleeting envy of braver cats. This mounting tension raises the question of whether he will break that comfortable chain or let it lead him to a gently wasted eighth life.

Philosophical Insights on Rejecting the Ordinary

Throughout history, many thinkers have urged us to escape the lull of average living, arguing that life's richness unfolds only when we stretch beyond the mundane. Felix, drifting in mediocrity, might benefit from these viewpoints if he can recall or discover them.

One classical influence is Aristotle, who taught the concept of virtue as a mean between extremes. At first glance, you might think settling for the middle is precisely what Felix is doing. But Aristotle's "golden mean" is not about seeking mediocrity; it is about finding balance in pursuit of excellence. Courage, for instance, stands between cowardice and recklessness yet remains a positive force that demands real bravery, not a halfway approach to fear.

Existential thinkers emphasise the idea of authenticity, creating meaning by fully inhabiting your choices. Mediocrity conflicts with authenticity because it often involves making the least demanding choices rather than those that align with your deeper convictions. If Felix took an existential view, he would see that living passively in "good enough" mode might contradict his innate desires, negating the responsibility he has to shape a purposeful existence.

Stoic philosophy also warns against complacency. While Stoics accept external events calmly, they encourage practising virtue and self-improvement daily. Felix's mild routine might appear Stoic at a casual glance, but genuine Stoics would question whether he is striving to refine his moral and practical capacities. If he is content to remain average, he is not embodying Stoic discipline.

Mediocrity

In many spiritual traditions, the path to enlightenment or deep wisdom involves persistent effort and introspection. A superficial life free of trials rarely yields profound insight. Felix, by choosing mediocrity, deprives himself of the testing ground that adversity and ambition might offer. Without challenges, the spiritual or intellectual breakthroughs that arise from perseverance elude him.

Meanwhile, self-help philosophies highlight the importance of a growth mindset. Accepting average as your peak can freeze your self-image. By seeing yourself as static, someone who is simply "not extraordinary", you block the upward spiral that continuous learning can spark. If Felix adopted a growth mindset, he would reframe his present average performance as just a step on a path of ongoing development rather than a final resting point.

Some collectivist philosophies emphasise that your personal excellence can uplift your community. Felix, settling for mediocrity, denies his neighbourhood the gifts he could bring if he pursued mastery or leadership. The ripple effect of someone pushing their potential can galvanise others to do likewise. If you have seen a workplace or team where one high performer raises the standard for everyone else, you know how powerful this dynamic can be.

On the flip side, a life of average sees no impetus for innovation or improvement. Philosophically, this can be seen as neglecting your inherent capacities. If existence is a precious chance to explore your talents and contribute meaningfully, mediocrity wastes that opportunity. Felix might reflect on how fleeting each life truly is. Does he really want to pass it in safe comfort, never learning what he is capable of?

Some philosophers also discuss the concept of eudaimonia, often translated as "flourishing." A flourishing life goes beyond mere contentment to embrace the realisation of your potential and the exercise of your best virtues. While Felix's eighth life is comfortable, it falls short of eudaimonia because he never pursues the fullness of his abilities. True flourishing demands engagement, challenge, and growth.

Ultimately, these philosophical strands converge on a message: contentment with mediocrity may shield you from risk but blocks the deeper rewards of excellence, creativity, and moral development. Felix, if he absorbed these ideas, might realise that simply avoiding pain or embarrassment is not the same as living richly. He could use them as a wake-up call, reminding him that each life is limited and that extraordinary outcomes arise only from extraordinary effort. The cost of ignoring this call is a bland existence, overshadowed by the possibility that he might have soared had he only tried.

Choosing Excellence Over the Comfort Zone

At some point, Felix's sense of gentle dissatisfaction crystallises. Perhaps he sees a younger cat break new ground with an innovative hunting strategy or notices a group of peers pursuing an ambitious project, returning home brimming with pride. He realises he has no equivalent achievements, only a series of safe, average days. This insight can spark a resolve to abandon mediocrity.

The first step is for Felix to define a bold goal, something beyond his current routine. Maybe he aims to master an advanced hunting technique, lead a small band to a distant territory, or forge alliances that demand real negotiation skills. By specifying an outcome that stretches him, he injects urgency and motivation into his daily life. You might parallel this in your journey: without a vision that challenges you, drifting in "fine" territory remains the default.

Next, he structures a plan to pursue this challenge. Mediocrity thrives on spontaneity and minimal effort, so Felix realises he must adopt a discipline that surpasses his usual comfortable pace. If, for instance, he wants to excel at hunting, he schedules regular practice sessions at times he used to lounge around. You might do likewise by setting aside consistent blocks for training or working on a demanding skill, ensuring progress even on days you do not feel particularly driven.

However, stepping beyond mediocrity brings friction. Felix's old friends, content in their average routines, might tease him or express disbelief. He faces pushback from the group that found his low-key presence reassuring. Some accuse him of arrogance for wanting more. Overcoming this social pressure requires inner conviction. If you have pursued a major life change, you know that others who prefer the status quo might resist or ridicule your ambitions.

Additionally, Felix must tackle his latent fear of failure. Mediocrity protected him from major disappointments. Now, striving for excellence opens the door to falling short. Yet he learns to reframe potential failure as learning rather than a catastrophe. Each stumbling step reveals new data, refining his technique or social approach. This shift from avoiding failure to embracing it as feedback can be pivotal in breaking free of "just enough."

Another crucial element is accountability. If Felix tries to cultivate advanced hunting alone, he may slack off when no one watches. Instead, he can partner with a cat who shares similar ambitions. They agree to meet each day, share progress, and push each other. You might replicate this strategy by finding a mentor, coach, or peer who keeps you honest about your goals. By reporting milestones or challenges, you maintain momentum.

Along the way, Felix reevaluates his relationships. If he aims to elevate his hunting or leadership skills, he may need to spend more time among cats with comparable drive. This does not mean abandoning old friends, but it does mean limiting how much he soaks in their complacent outlook. Building a supportive network that values excellence can accelerate his growth. The same applies to you; your environment can reinforce or undermine your pursuit of high-level goals.

A pivotal moment occurs when Felix experiences the thrill of real advancement. Maybe he completes a challenging hunt or negotiates a truce that benefits his group. That sense of pride far exceeds the mild contentment of average living. It affirms that stepping outside his comfort zone was worthwhile. This new high energises him, diminishing the appeal of safe mediocrity. Real success, even if modest, ignites a hunger to refine further.

It is not an easy path. Felix might face setbacks, injuries, or conflicts that test his resolve. He must reassert daily why he chose to aim higher. Doubt creeps in when progress stalls, or critics whisper that a comfortable, low-risk life was easier. By revisiting the philosophical insights about growth, authenticity, and potential, he can stay anchored in the belief that striving elevates not only himself but the community around him.

If Felix remains consistent, the final phase of transformation sees him more resilient, engaged, and creatively alive. He may not achieve flawless mastery or universal acclaim, but the difference from his mediocre days is stark. Instead of drifting in bland success, he experiences the vitality of purposeful action. Each new skill or alliance cements his sense that life is too short for half-hearted effort. The concluding weeks of his eighth life become a testament to the power of surpassing the ordinary. You, witnessing this change, might note how a few determined steps away from "adequate" can spark a cascade of breakthroughs.

In essence, choosing excellence over the comfort zone involves a clear goal, structured discipline, social support, reframed failure, and a willingness to face resistance. Felix's shift underscores that mediocrity is more than just a safe harbour, it is a subtle trap that drains ambition. Once he breaks free, he realises how much potential lay dormant behind the false security of "good enough." Whether he sustains this new zeal until the eighth life ends depends on ongoing vigilance. If he does, he will have learned a critical lesson: that surpassing mediocrity ignites a life worth remembering.

Conclusion of Eight Life

Felix's eighth life reveals that mediocrity, though outwardly stable and calm, quietly siphons off the chance for greatness. You have seen how ordinary goals keep him comfortable but unsatisfied. Without any glaring crises, Felix bobs along in safe routines, never discovering the thrill of extraordinary effort or the pride of skilful mastery. The hidden cost emerges in the slow erosion of ambition, creativity, and meaningful bonds.

Yet this chapter also shows that escaping mediocrity demands conscious choice. You must define a vision that stretches you, adopt daily discipline, and endure the discomfort of possible failure. This route is not easy, fellow cats might criticise your heightened aspirations, and part of you may fear the effort involved. Still, the rewards are profound: a deeper sense of achievement, richer relationships forged in shared striving, and the satisfaction of testing your real capabilities.

Watching Felix break free from "good enough" teaches you that life without challenge is ironically bland. Mediocrity can appear comforting in its stability, but it breeds a subtle restlessness and potential regret. When you dare to aim higher, you tap into reserves of skill, creativity, and resilience otherwise left dormant. In that choice, you transform an unremarkable existence into one charged with passion and possibility.

As Felix approaches the close of his eighth life, the real triumph is not whether he reaches a grand pinnacle, but that he rose above complacency to pursue a more daring path. Ask yourself now: is there an area where you have settled for average, telling yourself it is enough? If so, heed Felix's example. By challenging mediocrity, you rekindle the spark of genuine achievement, ensuring you do not look back one day and wonder what heights you might have reached if only you had tried.

The Ninth Life

Your Last Life

You have witnessed Felix confront eight distinct barriers: fear, comfort, procrastination, approval, aimlessness, regret, distraction, and mediocrity. In each life, he stumbled, discovered lessons, and tasted moments of clarity. Some challenges were dramatic, others discreet, yet all undermined his fullest potential. Now, arriving at his ninth and final life, Felix stands on the threshold of true transformation. Everything he has learned about courage, discipline, authenticity, purpose, forgiveness, focus, and ambition now forms the foundation for his greatest chapter.

In this last life, the stakes are higher than ever: no more second chances, no more quiet illusions that he can try again later. The call to live boldly and unapologetically has never been more urgent. Yet urgency alone is not enough. Felix must integrate every insight gleaned from his earlier pitfalls, weaving them into a cohesive daily practice that propels him beyond mere survival or average success.

This chapter guides you through the final stage of Felix's journey, showing how he embraces the urgency to leave a legacy that truly matters. You will see how daily habits define the difference between drifting and fulfilling a grand vision, how to link your aspirations with tangible impact, and why nothing short of wholehearted living will suffice when time is running out. Reflecting on Felix's evolution might stir you to ask: if this were your last life, would you approach your days any differently?

As you turn each page, you will glimpse the possibility of a ninth life in your own world, free from illusions, half-effort, or aimless wandering. The question is whether you will, like Felix, seize this final chance to make every moment count. A vibrant legacy awaits those who dare to live it, boldly, bravely, and without regret.

The Urgency to Live Boldly, Bravely, and Unapologetically

Felix enters his ninth life acutely aware of one truth: time is no longer a luxury. While each previous life taught him valuable lessons, he also clung to an unspoken safety net, the idea that if he failed or lingered too long in a trap, another chance would come. Now, that cushion is gone. With no more spare lives on the horizon, Felix feels a new intensity coursing through him. He can sense the clock ticking, and it stirs him to reevaluate how he spends every minute.

You might recognise this shift if you have ever confronted a life change or crisis that forced you to acknowledge life's brevity. Suddenly, the notion of "later" seems risky or even impossible. Felix realises that living boldly is not a whim, but a necessity if he hopes to harness the full potential he has so often postponed. What does boldness look like in practice? It means refusing to let fear of failure or judgement dictate your moves. It also means speaking your mind candidly, forging alliances that matter, and willingly risking short-term discomfort to secure a deeper sense of fulfilment.

Bravery, in this final life, extends beyond physical feats. Felix finds it in the willingness to be vulnerable with those who matter, to share his aspirations or regrets without hiding behind a façade. He sees how fear, examined in his first life, can still creep in subtly, urging him to keep his dreams modest. Yet remembering how fear once paralysed him, he chooses to face it head-on. Boldness, then, becomes an ongoing decision to move forward despite the flutter in his chest, to trust that every new leap can open doors he never suspected existed.

Being unapologetic means Felix stops seeking approval for every choice he makes. In the fourth life, chasing validation diluted his authenticity. Now, he stands firmly by his goals, acknowledging that not everyone will support or even understand him. This is especially true when your ambitions tower high, some cats may scoff or feel threatened. Felix commits to forging ahead anyway, realising that his final existence cannot be held captive by external opinions. In your own journey, you might recall how yearning for others' acceptance can sabotage true growth. Felix severs that tether, freeing himself to act from genuine conviction.

One might ask: why is urgency such a powerful force? It strips away excuses. When you believe you have endless tomorrows, procrastination becomes tempting. Felix once indulged that in his third life, letting tasks slide. Now, he sees no margin for delay. If an idea or opportunity appears, he either pursues it wholeheartedly or discards it consciously. He no longer clings to illusions of infinite do-overs. This clarity about time sharpens his daily decisions: each morning demands a purpose, each evening invites reflection on what was truly accomplished.

Such an outlook can be both liberating and daunting. Felix realises that if he wastes a day, he feels the loss keenly. Yet this sense of accountability fuels his determination. Rather than letting regret overshadow him, like in his sixth life, he harnesses that emotional weight as a motivational spark.

Whenever hesitation creeps in, he recalls the pain of regrets left unresolved, reminding himself that the cost of inaction is far greater than the risk of failure.

Moreover, urgency brings a new vibrancy to his encounters. Where he once might have chatted superficially, Felix now seeks genuine connection, asking deeper questions and revealing more of himself. This openness fosters richer bonds and more memorable moments. He knows he cannot afford shallow relationships or half-hearted commitments; in a final life, everything must be given the attention it deserves. Time spent with loved ones becomes precious, driving him to be fully present rather than distracted by trivial concerns.

Living boldly also means Felix demands more of himself physically and mentally. If he aims to become a master hunter, he trains diligently, refusing to settle for basic proficiency. If he sets out to explore distant territories, he does so wholeheartedly, leaving no corner uninvestigated. He realises that his capacity for achievement hinges on consistent effort, coasting through a day is no longer an option if he wants to embody the lessons of his eighth life, where mediocrity dulled his ambition.

In these daily acts of courage, Felix weaves together the wisdom from all prior lives. He wards off fear by trusting his resilience (Life 1), resists complacency by staying alert to comfort's silent traps (Life 2), conquers procrastination by acting now (Life 3), honours his own inner compass instead of chasing applause (Life 4), focuses on meaningful goals to avoid aimlessness (Life 5), forgives himself swiftly when mistakes happen to prevent regret (Life 6), cuts out distractions to maintain momentum (Life 7), and demands excellence instead of settling for average (Life 8). The synergy of these insights, combined with the pressing urgency of the ninth life, catapults him into a realm he has only glimpsed until now.

Ultimately, living boldly, bravely, and unapologetically is not about recklessness or relentless intensity every second. Felix still allows for rest, reflection, and spontaneous joys. But the difference is that his rest is purposeful; he recharges to fuel the next day's efforts, not to avoid them. His reflections are deep, integrating new lessons quickly instead of letting them stagnate. Spontaneous joys become opportunities for wholehearted engagement, not excuses to escape responsibility.

As you follow Felix into this final life, consider how your own sense of urgency might shift if you knew you had no other chances. Would you choose safer paths or let your convictions blaze a trail that, though perilous, leads to a more luminous end? The journey of this ninth life shows that genuine boldness can transform the ordinary into the extraordinary. In the face of ticking time, fear subsides, replaced by a raw determination to live as fully as possible.

The Daily Habits of Highly Effective and Impactful People

A grand vision, however urgent, falters without the support of consistent daily habits. Having embraced the final life's urgency, Felix soon discovers that lofty goals remain abstract unless converted into tangible routines. You might recall times when you felt surges of inspiration but failed to embed them in everyday practice, leading to fizzled dreams. For Felix, bridging this gap becomes essential if he wishes to leave a meaningful legacy.

First, he starts each morning with intentional planning. Rather than leaping into random tasks, he identifies one or two key actions that align with his overarching goals. If his aim is to cultivate leadership among neighbouring cats, for example, he plans a brief meeting or training session. If mastering advanced hunting is on the agenda, he commits to practising certain techniques at a set time. This habit counters the drift that once plagued him in earlier lives. As you may have experienced, a focused morning routine can anchor your entire day, preventing aimless wandering.

Next, Felix prioritises energy management. He recalls how procrastination (Life 3) and distraction (Life 7) often emerged when he was tired or unmotivated. Now, he ensures adequate rest, mindful nutrition, and short, energising breaks. This might look like a midday pause for a quiet reflection or a brisk, purposeful walk around the territory. You, too, might find that small rituals to restore energy significantly boost consistency. Felix learns that, in a final life, you cannot rely on sporadic bursts of enthusiasm; stable energy underpins daily achievement.

Effective people also carve out deep work periods. Felix remembers the days he scattered his attention among countless trivial amusements. Now, he sets aside blocks of time for uninterrupted focus, switching off from casual social chatter or lesser tasks. Whether practising advanced hunting drills or strategising for community improvements, he immerses himself fully. This deep work concept, emphasised by productivity experts, ensures that each session yields tangible progress. Doing so daily transforms a vague ambition into steady, measurable gains.

Another crucial habit is reflective journaling, or in Felix's case, a quiet mental recap. Each evening, he notes what went well, what he learned, and where he stumbled. This practice cements lessons faster, preventing repeated mistakes. It also fosters humility, reminding him that even in a final life, there is always room for improvement. If you adopt a similar habit, you might be surprised how quickly your self-awareness sharpens, making each day an iterative step forward rather than a random cycle of activity.

Collaboration plays a key role. Felix realises that truly impactful cats do not act alone. He forms a small circle of peers who share his vision, maybe improving hunting techniques for the younger generation or stabilising local territories. They hold each other accountable, celebrate wins, and troubleshoot setbacks. This communal approach counters the isolation he once felt in certain lives, reinforcing a sense of shared responsibility. Humans often mirror this by joining masterminds or support groups that elevate everyone's standards. Teamwork multiplies the effect of each individual's daily habits.

Moreover, effective people avoid decision fatigue by simplifying minor choices. Felix picks a consistent route for his morning patrol, a standard approach to certain tasks, and a fixed schedule for essential duties. This frees mental bandwidth for more creative or challenging decisions. If you have ever ended a day frazzled by a thousand tiny choices, you know how such friction drains your capacity for strategic thinking. Felix learns that in a time-limited life, preserving mental clarity is vital.

Connected to this is the habit of delegation or graceful refusal. Felix no longer tries to handle every small matter. If a trivial argument arises among younger cats, he might delegate it to a promising mentor he has been training. By reserving his energy for tasks aligned with his core goals, he ensures meaningful impact instead of dissipating himself across myriad minor disputes. You might consider a similar approach to emails, errands, or social obligations that dilute your prime time. Focusing only on what uniquely demands your attention accelerates progress.

Effective individuals also maintain a growth mindset, never settling even after success. Felix realises that complacency nearly trapped him in his eighth life. Now, each milestone triggers a question: "How can I refine this further?" This does not mean perpetual dissatisfaction but rather a healthy, ongoing curiosity. If he masters one advanced hunting technique, he seeks the next. If his leadership project stabilises a territory, he ponders the next step in community development. In your own pursuits, this mindset fosters continuous evolution rather than a peak-and-plateau pattern.

Felix couples all this with unwavering kindness and empathy. Observing the pitfalls of seeking approval (Life 4) or living aimlessly (Life 5), he notes that daily impact arises from truly caring about others' growth, too. He invests time in guiding those who approach him, encouraging them to adopt structured habits themselves. This fosters a ripple effect: each cat who learns from Felix's example might pass on the discipline to another, compounding the community's overall improvement.

Lastly, Felix keeps the bigger picture in view. Every morning routine, deep work session, or reflection exercise is not an end in itself, but a brick laid toward a future legacy. He envisions how his final life can reshape the territory for years to come, even after he is gone. This sense of long-range vision helps him persist when daily tasks feel tedious or challenging. By tying near-term habits to a grand objective, he transforms routine into a noble endeavour. If you have a similarly grand dream, linking minor actions to that overarching purpose can boost your motivation far beyond short-term impulse.

In sum, the daily habits of highly effective and impactful people revolve around planning, energy management, deep focus, reflective learning, strategic collaboration, simplified decisions, growth-mindedness, compassion, and the unifying sense of a larger mission. As Felix embraces these patterns, he sees his final life swiftly blossoming with tangible achievements. Each day's consistent, purposeful effort accumulates, weaving a narrative of steady transformation that dwarfs any fleeting excitement he once chased in lesser lives. Through these habits, you too can bridge the gap between lofty intentions and real-world impact, proving that even a single life, final or otherwise, can leave an enduring mark.

Leaving a Lasting Legacy: How to Ensure Your Life Truly Matters

Even as Felix refines his daily habits, a question looms: what does it mean to leave a legacy? In earlier lives, he chased fleeting triumphs or social approval, but neither provided a timeless imprint. Now, with the ninth life ending his nine-lives cycle, Felix seeks something more enduring, an impact that will outlast his physical presence.

Legacy, in his eyes, begins with identifying what truly resonates at the intersection of personal passion and communal need. If fear once reigned, or comfort lulled him, or mediocrity tamed him, now he fights to ensure that no ephemeral distraction diverts him from tackling a domain that matters deeply. For Felix, this might mean ensuring the next generation of cats inherits a safer, better-organised territory. Or it could be pioneering advanced knowledge in hunting or resource management that future cats can build upon. You might find your own calling in parallel, noticing where your unique strengths solve pressing problems.

Felix also learns that legacy is not solely about big gestures. Sometimes the greatest legacies emerge from teaching, mentoring, or quietly improving daily life for others. He might help a struggling cat gain confidence to thrive independently or unify small groups to maintain a stable environment. These may not earn him widespread renown, yet they plant seeds that can flourish after he departs. Humans often see legacy as grand monuments or famous accolades, but behind the scenes, countless unsung heroes lay the groundwork that shapes future generations.

A critical element is consistency. An isolated noble deed rarely cements a legacy; rather, repeated acts of service or leadership create a lasting impression. Felix realises that daily discipline, kindness, and strategic thinking must persist over weeks, months, and beyond. This mirrors how lasting human innovations or social progress typically arise: not from one grand stroke, but from sustained effort by dedicated individuals. In your realm, legacies form where determined hearts persist in the face of apathy or resistance.

Moreover, leaving a legacy demands letting go of ego. Felix notes how approval-seeking (Life 4) and vanity can distort pure intentions. If he craves recognition, he risks undermining genuine collaboration or overshadowing others' contributions. Instead, he cultivates humility, focusing on results rather than acclaim. This stance fosters trust and encourages others to step up. By minimising personal glory, Felix ensures that systems, knowledge, or alliances continue functioning effectively after he is gone, rather than collapsing around a single charismatic figure.

This approach also invites cooperation. A single cat cannot alone shape a territory's future. Felix identifies allies who share his vision, delegating responsibilities in ways that empower them. Through mutual respect, he avoids the trap of distraction or micromanagement. You might replicate this by assembling a trustworthy team for any large endeavour, ensuring each person feels valued and prepared to carry on if you must step aside.

Mentorship further cements Felix's legacy. He invests time mentoring younger cats who show promise. This does more than pass along skills; it embeds a mindset of excellence, resilience, and compassion that can outlast him. In a human context, think of educators or mentors who shaped your trajectory long after you parted ways. Their influence persists precisely because they cultivated your capacity to continue evolving on your own. Felix, too, aims to foster self-sustaining progress.

Another dimension involves documenting knowledge. Felix realises that each generation can lose vital insights if they are not consistently recorded or passed on. While cats might not write books, they can share formalised methods or oral teachings that the group memorises. If you have a special area of expertise, writing or producing materials ensures your ideas remain accessible to others. For Felix, establishing a clear set of guidelines or communal practices can be an enduring gift.

Moreover, Felix addresses conflict resolution. He foresees that future territorial disputes could undo much of his work if no framework for cooperation exists. By creating stable, fair systems to handle disagreements, he provides a template that fosters harmony long after his final breath. You might see parallels in organisational leadership, where shaping a constructive culture outlasts any individual leader's tenure.

A lasting legacy also calls for generosity of spirit. Felix, reflecting on past regrets, commits to open-handedly sharing resources, knowledge, and opportunities. This generosity does not deplete him; rather, it multiplies the positive effect. Others, benefitting from his readiness to help, replicate that ethic. The territory evolves toward mutual support instead of scarcity-driven rivalries. In your own sphere, a legacy of kindness might overshadow any single accomplishment, ensuring you are remembered not just for what you did, but for how you made people feel.

Finally, Felix realises that a genuine legacy often emerges quietly. He might never see the full fruits of his labour. Perhaps future generations of cats will refine his methods, rename them, and scarcely recall he was the origin. Yet the essence of his contribution remains woven into their daily life, whether they know it or not. This is the humbling truth of real impact: the best legacies often transcend personal recognition, continuing in ways the originator could not have predicted.

In embracing this perspective, Felix frees himself from any last vestiges of vanity or impatience. He devotes himself to the cause, trusting that seeds sown today will blossom tomorrow, even if he is not there to witness the bloom. For you, this means focusing on depth, consistency, mentorship, documentation, and communal structures that persist independently of your presence. The measure of success is not immediate applause, but the enduring transformation left in your wake.

Thus, leaving a lasting legacy means forging a path that others can follow and build upon. Felix's final life proves that a genuine, far-reaching impact does not rely on an infinite timeline; sometimes, working with urgency and clarity yields a more focused, integrated contribution than decades of drifting. Each action in these final days resonates beyond him, ensuring that long after he is gone, the territory and the hearts of those within it bear the imprint of his devoted vision.

Tying It All Together: Lessons from Lives 1-8

As Felix integrates his daily habits and clarifies the legacy he hopes to leave, he finds himself reflecting on every life that led him here. Each of the eight previous incarnations, with all their pitfalls and revelations, forms a puzzle piece in the grand mosaic of his personal evolution. When he aligns them, he realises how each stage contributed something indispensable to his final stride toward fulfilment.

The First Life taught him about fear, showing that unchecked anxiety can immobilise ambition. Now, facing the final life, Felix no longer hides from challenges. Instead, he channels the adrenaline of fear into calculated risk-taking. This practice preserves the caution that fear can provide while preventing paralysis. In your own trajectory, you might recall that acknowledging fear without letting it dictate your actions liberates you to aim higher.

From the Second Life, where comfort lulled him, he retains vigilance against complacency. Whenever a pleasant routine tempts him to stall, he recalls how a life of perpetual comfort ultimately fosters stagnation. Thus, in the ninth life, short rests serve to recharge, not to entrench him in a safe bubble. That distinction helps him balance well-being with drive. Humans often mirror this by ensuring self-care does not devolve into chronic avoidance of growth.

Procrastination from the Third Life shaped Felix's sense of time. He no longer postpones vital tasks. Instead, he frontloads important actions early in the day or week, aware that delayed beginnings rarely see satisfying endings. This shift kills the inertia that once sapped his potential. If you have also battled procrastination, you know how deciding to "do it now" transforms vague dreams into accomplished milestones.

Life 4's chase for approval taught Felix the hollowness of shaping your path around others' applause. Now, while he cherishes genuine camaraderie and feedback, he no longer contorts his mission to please the crowd. This newfound authenticity preserves his goals from external distortions, letting him move confidently even if some cats fail to understand or support his direction. Similarly, you may find that relinquishing the need for universal acceptance unlocks the courage to pursue your true calling.

Aimlessness in Life 5 revealed the vacuum created by drifting without purpose. In the final life, Felix ensures each day ties back to a clear vision. If he plans a territory-wide improvement, each morning includes tangible steps that accumulate toward that outcome. This approach wards off the emptiness of aimless wandering, providing a consistent sense of momentum. Humans often experience this as well, realising that a personal mission statement can anchor everyday choices in a bigger narrative.

From the Sixth Life, he remembers the weight of regret. Rather than letting missed chances haunt him, he chooses to act promptly, expressing gratitude, forging alliances, or finishing tasks that might otherwise linger. This decisiveness liberates him from revisiting regrets in the future. You might adopt a similar stance, deciding that regret is an urgent signal to do better immediately instead of brooding over past omissions.

Life 7's battle with distraction taught Felix the necessity of deep focus. So in the ninth life, he invests in mindful concentration on tasks that matter, ignoring trivial lures. This consistent attention helps him produce quality work and deeper connections. People frequently discover that limiting distractions, be they digital or social, elevates their daily output far beyond quick, scattered efforts.

Finally, mediocrity in Life 8 highlighted how "good enough" quietly drains ambition. To avoid that grey plateau, Felix continuously calibrates his goals upward. Each time he achieves a milestone, he raises the bar slightly, ensuring that complacency does not creep back in. Humans often find that once they achieve a moderate success, the temptation to rest on those laurels is strong; refusing that lull keeps the growth curve ascending.

Tying these eight lessons together, Felix realises they form a framework for a life of true excellence and contribution:

1. **Harness Fear**: Let it warn you of real danger, but never let it block your ambitions.

2. **Shatter Comfort**: Treat rest as a tool for recovery, not a perpetual retreat from new challenges.
3. **Stop Delays**: If it matters, do it without waiting for a perfect moment.
4. **Seek Authenticity**: Chart a course based on conviction, not applause.
5. **Cultivate Purpose**: Let each choice echo a larger vision that resonates with your identity.
6. **Convert Regret**: Use sorrow for missed chances to motivate swift and decisive action now.
7. **Guard Your Attention**: Focus deeply to build mastery rather than scattering energy on trifles.
8. **Refuse Mediocrity**: Aim beyond the ordinary, for "just fine" saps the thrill of exceeding limits.

He sees these eight pillars as a compass guiding him through the final life's labyrinth of decisions and challenges. Instead of wandering as in previous incarnations, he systematically applies each principle, forging an unshakeable foundation that stands up to every temptation or setback. In your own life, you may do likewise, reviewing past phases or mistakes to identify the guiding lessons they offer, then using them as a blueprint for present and future actions.

The synergy of these lessons is greater than the sum of its parts. Any single one, like controlling fear or refining focus, brings improvement, but weaving them all together yields exponential transformation. Felix experiences how, each time he edges near complacency, one of the lessons jolts him awake. When fear tries to reassert itself, he draws on the memory of successful bravery. When doubt creeps in, he trusts the discipline of daily practice to pave the way. If a fleeting desire for comfort surfaces, he recalls how Life 2 led to a dead-end.

Thus, by unifying the insights of Lives 1–8, Felix stands ready to face the culminating demands of Life 9. No single flaw can now topple him, because he has encountered them all and learned how to respond. The question that remains is how effectively he will combine these lessons in real time, under the pressure of the final countdown. If he does so consistently, he can avoid repeating old patterns, forging instead a grand combination of growth, resilience, and purpose. If you do the same with your own past lessons, you might find that even the gravest errors become stepping stones toward a future that surpasses your prior limits.

The Final Awakening: Embracing Your Last Life's Legacy

In the twilight of his ninth life, Felix senses a profound shift. Each day resonates with significance as he applies the eight hard-won lessons to every decision. The synergy between urgency, daily habits, legacy-building, and integrated wisdom makes this final chapter of his existence the most impactful by far. Yet, even as he moves forward, one lingering element remains: the final awakening, a deep realisation that transcends the mechanics of success and touches the essence of who he has become.

This awakening begins when Felix contemplates mortality without fear or regret. In the past, he either dreaded loss or felt sorrow over what he never accomplished. Now, he stands at peace with the knowledge that life ends. Instead of gloom, he feels gratitude. Each moment is an unrepeatable gift, so he invests himself wholly. This perspective intensifies the vibrancy of ordinary tasks: a simple hunt under the moonlight, a heartfelt conversation with a friend, or a silent gaze at a sunrise. You might find that embracing finiteness in your own life transforms mundane routines into experiences brimming with wonder.

Emotional freedom emerges as well. No longer bound by the pursuit of others' approval, Felix expresses joy, sorrow, or empathy without reservation. He sees vulnerability not as weakness but as a conduit for genuine connection. Past regrets no longer haunt him, for he is actively forging new memories that overshadow old wounds. Ambition does not become arrogance because he recalls the humbling lessons of regret, fear, and mediocrity, ensuring humility in every stride. You, too, might find that self-acceptance and open-heartedness blossom when you integrate your entire life history into a coherent present-day identity.

Another layer of awakening involves unconditional commitment to his chosen path. Felix no longer dithers or second-guesses. If he decides a certain territorial reform is vital, he pursues it unwaveringly, adapting tactics but never losing sight of the goal. This unwavering stance stands in stark contrast to the aimlessness or distraction of earlier lives. It is not stubbornness but clarity. He has teased out what matters from the swirl of possibilities, discarding the rest. Humans in a parallel journey often realise that true mastery or influence arises only when you concentrate on a few worthy aims instead of scattering effort across countless trivial endeavours.

Felix also rediscovers wonder. In the rush toward big achievements, it is easy to become fixated on tasks and goals, forgetting the raw beauty in each day. Yet now, ironically, the final sense of urgency makes him more attuned to simple miracles: the intricate pattern on a leaf, the comforting warmth of a friend by his side, or the silent majesty of a star-lit sky. This awakened wonder energises him, countering any risk of burnout from constant striving. If you have ever paused in a hectic schedule to truly marvel at a sunset, you have touched the essence of this feeling, one that balances ambition with reverence for life's inherent poetry.

Community transformation accelerates during this phase, largely due to Felix's unwavering focus and the example he sets. Younger cats watch him tackle challenges with courage and discipline, absorbing his methods and mindset. Allies who once harboured scepticism soften as they witness the tangible outcomes of his leadership. The territory begins to shift, fewer squabbles erupt, resources are managed more fairly, and collaborations spark unexpected innovations. Felix sees that his personal awakening ripples outward, changing the environment in ways that may outlast him.

Near the end of his ninth life, Felix experiences a quiet sense of completion. It is not that he has done everything possible, nor that there are no remaining struggles. Rather, it is the knowledge that he has poured himself into each day with authenticity. Every mistake he made served a lesson, every triumph shaped new possibilities, and every interaction contributed to a communal legacy. He can depart without the shadow of "what if" because he has confronted each of his personal demons and integrated their teachings into a cohesive approach to living.

You might ask: "What is the final takeaway for me?" The answer resides in the idea that every day can be lived as if it were part of a final life. The clarity Felix gains from realising time is finite can guide you now. You need not wait for a dire situation or an ultimate life-limiting moment to apply these principles of bold living, daily discipline, legacy-building, integrated wisdom, and awakened gratitude. Instead, you can adopt them as the cornerstones of your current path, ensuring that regrets do not pile up unchecked, that comfortable mediocrity never caps your true capabilities, and that fear or external validation do not sabotage your self-authorship.

The final awakening is a sense of purposeful serenity. Felix transitions from chasing success to embodying it, from fearing judgment to radiating self-trust, from drifting among distractions to embracing unwavering focus. All eight lessons converge into a single, elegantly woven ethos: live each day with courage, authenticity, discipline, vision, forgiveness, attentiveness, and excellence. When he strings these virtues together, the sum transforms his life's narrative from a cautionary tale into an inspiring testimony.

As the last day draws near, Felix does not panic. He has cultivated the daily habits of effective living, shaped a legacy that stands on more than fleeting achievements and anchored himself in the principles gleaned from each life's mistakes. Rather than lamenting the end, he savours the completion of a story well-told. In the final act, what glows brightest is not a single heroic deed but the sum of consistent, heartfelt choices that define who he has become. For you, the lesson is clear: if you weave your own life with the same deliberate threads, you may find that any final curtain call feels less like a tragic ending and more like a triumphant finale.

Conclusion

Now you have walked with Felix from his first, fearful steps to his ninth and final life, where he integrates every hard-won lesson. Fear taught him courage; comfort taught him vigilance against stagnation; procrastination showed him time's fragility; approval-chasing led him back to authenticity; aimlessness sharpened the value of purpose; regret energised him to act while he still could; distraction proved the power of focused attention; and mediocrity pushed him to demand excellence. These insights culminate in a final awakening that fuses urgency, discipline, legacy, and wonder into a life worth celebrating.

Felix's ninth life is urgent, yet not frantic; bold, yet not reckless; purposeful, yet not rigid. He invests each day in meaningful habits that serve a grander vision, forging bonds, and leaving footprints that persist beyond his final breath. In this closing chapter, he demonstrates that real transformation is possible when you refuse half-measures, integrate past lessons, and embrace your journey with unwavering intention.

For you, this final life stands as an invitation. If you have ever postponed a dream or let old failures discourage you, consider Felix's story a nudge to act now. Harness fear instead of letting it immobilise you; replace comfort-seeking with growth; conquer procrastination through daily action; free yourself from others' approval; craft a compelling mission; use regret as momentum, not a millstone; reclaim your focus; and rise above the mundane. In doing so, you might discover the true breadth of your capabilities.

The 9th Life of Felix The Cat

Let the ninth life remind you that no day is guaranteed, no talent should lie dormant, and no calling is too lofty. Ultimately, it is now or never, time to abandon excuses and half-hearted living. Like Felix, you can transform your final stretch, whatever it may be, into a beacon of purpose, creativity, and lasting impact. Your legacy awaits, ready to be forged by each deliberate choice you make today.